44 HOURS & 21 MINUTES
A WOMAN'S TRUTH AND POWER

44 HOURS & 21 MINUTES

A WOMAN'S TRUTH AND POWER

RASHAWN RENÉE

REAL TRUTH INTERNATIONAL LLC

44 HOURS & 21 MINUTES

A Woman's Truth and Power

ISBN   978-1-5445-0080-5 *Hardcover*

978-1-5445-0078-2 *Paperback*

978-1-5445-0077-5 *Ebook*

978-1-5445-0079-9 *Audiobook*

This book is dedicated to a woman who has made the choice
to learn her real truth and live powerfully. She is resilient,
devoted, and tireless in the pursuit to live the life of her dreams.
She is a woman who demonstrates love-of-self and family
in all she does. She is my cheerleader and quiet strength.

She is our mother.

* * * *

Thank you, Mom, for believing in me and choosing to
excavate and become a more extraordinary woman.

CONTENTS

Note: This book shares some of my life and offers insights, perspective, and invites the reader to learn more about themselves. I have changed identifying characteristics and details such as locations, occupations, and some names in order to maintain anonymity of people and places.

FOREWORD

I call RaShawn Renée Dr. Capable! She is powerful, courageous, joyful, compassionate, and mindful, with an evolved higher consciousness that is changing the world.

As readers go through RaShawn Renée's life journey in *44 Hours & 21 Minutes: A Woman's Truth and Power*, they will have a unique opportunity and invitation to travel with her and see for themselves who she is. She's a fully integrated, evolved human being, with her soul, heart, mind, and body cross-fertilizing each aspect of being human.

RaShawn Renée speaks real truth and invites the reader to go deep within themselves to touch their real truth. Such a journey leads to real power that resides within every one of us. Such power can never be taken from us because it is not dependent on outside circumstances or other people. And such real power leads to real inner peace and joyfulness, no matter what external situations or circumstances we find ourselves in, so writes RaShawn Renée.

In *44 Hours & 21 Minutes: A Woman's Truth and Power*, she shows us how she gained her real power by questioning what she once believed in and how she acquired her beliefs. She asks the reader to do the same. How much of what you believe in is your conditioning? When we carefully examine this question, we realize our beliefs are not inherent to who we are, but are often someone else's ideas of who we should be. All the conditioning we experience, long before we are even conscious beings, becomes our ways of thinking, feeling, and acting. The price is surrendering our own real truth and real power that resides in all of us and can be excavated and revealed. By reading and practicing RaShawn Renée's directives, we will live a more fulfilling life in every way possible, just as we were created to do.

44 Hours & 21 Minutes: A Woman's Truth and Power, provides us with the opportunity to delve inside our conditioning and evolve by revealing who we really are. RaShawn Renée is on a mission to impact at least 111,000,000 women, beginning with you and creating a ripple effect that will make the world a better place for

everyone. The change begins with us, as I have learned
from this author.

STEPHEN SALTZMAN, PHD

PROFESSOR EMERITUS OF PSYCHOLOGY

Love Note from RaShawn Renée

Happy Love Day!

Hello dear precious and cherished woman

Today is the day that you, me and each person who has read "44 hours & 21 minutes, A Woman's Truth and Power" bonds through Love. Meaning, when another person reads and applies their learning, there is more love revealed in the world... Thank You for contributing.

The communications in this book through stories and inquiries are my learning and discoveries. My intention is to assist you in living a life filled/felt with more love through real Truth and Power.

Being a woman is magnificent, challenging and an honor. With this female gender, we've been given or chosen comes a power that many of us aren't aware or rarely think about.

Consider this...we perpetuate society and without us human kind would perish.

We are resilient and capable. We intrinsically know how to lead and govern.

As you read this book, please know that you are unique, remarkable and definitely **the Prize**!

Only Love,
RR

PART I

THE SEEDING
&
THE DISCOVERY

CHAPTER ONE

―――――

YES FOR THE FIRST TIME

It was one of the most regal homes in the neighborhood. It sat poised and dignified on a corner lot, like a queen sitting on her throne. Its cobblestone entry was inviting, nestled behind a white picket fence with perfectly appointed gardenias, a manicured lawn, and a sprawling front porch. The visual appeal and alluring fragrances were hypnotic, proclaiming: *You have arrived. This is where you want to be.*

"People work all their lives, dreaming to have some of this, and you've got it all." Those were my biological father's words the first time he saw the house. I wasn't certain if it was pride, wonderment, or something else. I told myself he was proud, pleased, and impressed with the house that was to be my home.

I was a grown woman making another conscious vow of silence. I chose not to tell him the truth or, perhaps better stated, not to tell him the story of what I was enduring in that exquisite house while in a relationship with a man who thought I would be his wife and who had become my captor. I made the conscious and conditioned choice to stay silent. It was very important to me that my father and everyone else had the thoughts that my life was good. I wanted him and others to be proud of me. I needed him to think everything was perfect, and I hoped he would be excited about my life, because then, perhaps, he would be a consistent part of my life.

Looking back, I don't know if I could have articulated the reality of my situation. However, what I do know is that I could have told what was occurring, yet I didn't.

I was a woman who kept secrets to protect her image and those close to her. How did I become that woman, a woman who pretended to have it all together while feeling absent from Self?

People told me from a young age, "You talk too much." I, like every child (until taught differently), was naturally curious about everything and asked questions to develop an understanding. I often had questions relating to the stark divide of behavior between the men and women within my environment. The observations constantly supported the ideology that women are subservient to men and a man's happiness is paramount to all else within the family. I would take my questions to anyone in the family who I thought could answer. "Why can't I go to the ranch anymore with Grandpa?" "Why is Grandma mad at me?" These were two of the many questions I asked often. I was told to be quiet and to stop asking so many questions. I learned over time that the adults were often lying when I asked questions that would prompt answers which would have contradicted the harmonious and inclusive perception of the family they were promoting. My continual observations, questioning, and responses eventually led me to silence while trying to accept what was. My voice was silent, and after a while, the new inquiry within the family was, "Why aren't you talking? What's wrong with you?"

Growing up and curiosity go hand-in-hand with the ability to learn and gain understanding. In childhood, our natural curiosity can be diminished by the need for belonging and feeling cared for. The emotional unfoldment of our primary years clearly conveys the message we want to belong and be loved. It's our natural inclination to seek and need truth. When a child is encouraged to be silent instead of curious and engaged, it can have compounding adverse effects that can last over decades or even a lifetime.

The first time I made the conscious vow to be silent occurred when I was a young girl. The vow was a by-product of conditioning to survive and satisfy the need to feel as if I belonged.

One of my favorite pastimes was going to the family ranch with my grandpa and his friends. I had so much fun at the ranch. It was my special time with Grandpa. Usually on the drive to the ranch, at some point after we exited the last well-paved road, my grandfather would put me on his lap and let me drive the truck with him. He was my buddy, protector, had confidence in my abilities, and was the man I trusted. When at the ranch, I could do whatever I wanted. I thought I was the most important person around when I was with Grandpa, because he made everyone cater to my every request. He was a leader, always seemed to be enjoying himself, and everyone acquiesced to him. I felt special knowing I was the apple of his eye and the focus of much of his attention. So, his eventual upset with me, which was the result of me talking too much, greatly influenced my choice to be silent.

Each time we arrived at the ranch, I would first go to the chickens, rabbits, goats, and other animals and play with my nonhuman best friends before setting off on an adventure in nature to play for hours. I had mountains, rocks, trees, a lake, and all the freedom I wanted. Grandpa constantly reinforced in me that I could do anything I set out to do. When I asked if I could climb what seemed like the biggest tree in the world he said, "If you think you can climb it, climb it, and if you need me, I'm here." That was pretty much his attitude with me regarding everything. So when I heard, "No! You can't go with me this time, and I'm not taking you anymore," I couldn't believe the words that had come from his mouth. I said, "Daddy (my nickname for Grandpa), I want to go!"

"No! You're not going with me anymore!" he said. I left the room, went to the patio, and tried to figure out what I had done wrong. Why wasn't my buddy, my grandfather, smiling at me, and why did he say no? As I heard him go out the front door, I ran from the patio and down the driveway, so I could meet him at the truck. When I got there, he was loading the back of the truck. "I want to go," I said again. "Mama (one of his many nicknames for me), you're not going with me. You talk too much," he replied. He got in the truck, told me he would bring me something back, smiled, and backed out of the driveway. I stood there sad and bewildered. Then I walked to the end of the driveway until I could no longer see the truck. A couple times he waved from the window, so I had the hope he would change his mind, turn around, come back, and take me with him. However, that didn't happen. Tears ran down my face as I walked back up the driveway and sat on the porch. This was my first real punishment, and I had no idea what I had said or done. Yet, I was being punished by someone I trusted and who thought I was special. My buddy, my grandfather, my protector left me and told me "No" for the first time, and it was because I talked too much.

I sat on the porch for what seemed like hours, tears streaming down my face, hoping that my grandpa would return for me. Once I accepted he wasn't coming back, I wiped my tears and went back into the house. I was headed to my bedroom when I saw my uncle and cousin playing chess.

My uncle asked, "What's wrong with you?"

I said, "Daddy didn't let me go with him to the ranch because I talk too much."

"You do talk too much, and you need to stay out of grown folks' business," he responded.

From that point, I learned to be silent and suppress the urge within to speak out in any way that might upset the desires, expectations, or harmony of the adults. An addendum to my silence also stifled my urge to share my feelings unless they conformed with the perception of how I was supposed to feel.

One evening, while my grandfather was away at the ranch without me, I overheard my uncle on the phone telling someone why I wasn't at the ranch. I learned from listening what caused my grandfather to take away my visits with him to the ranch. My uncle spoke of a conversation I'd had with my grandmother regarding a recent trip I'd taken with Grandpa to the ranch. While talking to my grandmother about the fun I'd had with Grandpa, I also included the fun I'd had with his lady friend. Of course, I didn't know that telling of my adventures and fun would present a problem for Grandpa. As I listened to my uncle's conversation, I still didn't understand what was wrong or bad about what I'd told my grandmother. Yet, from my uncle's tone, I knew I'd done something really bad.

According to my uncle, when my grandmother questioned my grandfather about my story regarding our time together at the ranch, Grandpa said, "She wasn't telling the truth. She must have been playing pretend." While listening to my uncle, I recalled that while sharing my story with my grandmother, she became very sad. I thought her sadness was because she wanted to be with us, so I invited her to go with us more often. I also remembered that when Grandpa came home from work that day, the two of them got into an argument. While arguing, they called me into their bedroom. My grandmother asked me to tell her about how my grandfather, his lady friend, and I had slept at the ranch. I told her I slept in my own room, not with Grandpa and his friend. My grandfather told me to leave the room. As I was leaving, I heard him say, "She doesn't know what she's talking about."

Overhearing my uncle's conversation, recalling the sadness of my grandmother, the argument between my grandparents, and feeling the sting of not being able to go to the ranch with my grandfather, all of these fed the unconscious training and conditioning for me to be silent, not to trust my words, because they could cause sadness and hurt people I cared about.

The conditioning of silence is insidious, and at first glance, it would appear my conditioning began in childhood. However, it began when I was still in my mother's womb. Do you know when yours began? My precious young mother gave her virginity and became pregnant with me. The perceived shame cast upon the family was more than my grandmother could bear, so she, my grandmother, wanted to have me aborted and eventually moved my mother across town with another family, where no one knew my mother or our family. My mother's pregnancy as I developed in her womb was cloaked with secrets, silence, and being hidden. I was born prematurely, probably due to the stress and trauma my mother was experiencing as a result of all the turmoil surrounding her pregnancy. After being discharged from the hospital, I was taken to my grandparents' home, where there was a familial culture among the women of being silent, keeping secrets, and maintaining appropriate appearances. It was also a place where we learned to take care of one another. I am aware my mother and I both could have been wholly dismantled emotionally; however, we weren't, and she and I have learned to be seen, be heard, and use every experience in our life for upliftment. In the home where I grew up, everyone was doing the best they knew how to, and gave me and my mother the love of their understanding.

In our home lived my mother, her parents (my grandparents), her grandmother (my great-grandmother), her brother (my uncle), her sister (my aunt), and various cousins, great-aunts, great-uncles, and family friends who needed a place to live. My grandparents were financially successful and believed charity began with family. They often helped family members relocate, purchase their first homes, get jobs, or start their own businesses. I was raised to give, contribute, and share.

My biological parents never married, but when I was four, my mother married the man who raised me, and we became a family. We moved from my grandparents' home to another city. It seemed like a world away from my grandparents. Half the time, I still stayed with my grandparents, and the other half with my mother and bonus father. I felt like a welcomed visitor in both places. The messaging of we take care of one another, communication with discernment according to a given situation, concealing socially unacceptable truths, and that men have all the power was passed on to me while growing up. That's a lot to unpack as a child, yet it is all part of my former conditioning.

Do you know what you need to unpack?

Have you ever taken the time to reflect on the messaging passed on to you?

❊   ❊   ❊   ❊

It's hard to recall a time as a child when I didn't get cuddles or a back rub to help me fall asleep. At ten, all that changed. It was early morning, and I was awakened by unfamiliar sounds. I immediately felt scared and knew to be silent. I lay there, pretending to still be asleep. I heard panting, heavy breathing, and then a sigh. Shortly after the sigh, the man got out of my bed. I lay there for a while, afraid to move. When I finally turned over, I smelled something strange. I wasn't sure exactly what had happened, but I felt it was bad. I got out of bed and left my room. I didn't know what to do or whom to tell. I was afraid of telling and scared not to tell. When I left my room, I quietly and cautiously checked the house to see if he was still there. He wasn't. So I did nothing except make the choice not to tell (I talked too much). Over the next few days, I slept on alert, meaning I barely slept. Every sound made me wake up and check my surroundings. It was about a week later when he came into my room again. This time, I saw him open his pants and pull out his penis, although I pretended like I was asleep. I don't recall seeing a man's penis prior to that experience. Unlike the first time, I wished I was dead, because being dead would be easier than telling. I was traumatized! I thought I could kill myself or tell. Obviously, I didn't kill myself, and I really wanted to tell my grandfather, but he was traveling. I couldn't take being silent anymore. So I went to my mother, feeling consumed with this confusion, bewilderment, having thoughts of death, and feeling shame. I sheepishly told her my experience of how the man came into my room and masturbated twice. "Are you sure?" she said while crying and trembling. "Are you OK? Did he do anything else?" she asked. Then she declared with the strength of a lioness, "Don't worry. I'll take care of this."

The day after I told my mom, I saw the man, and from somewhere within, I had the courage to say to him, "If you ever take out your private parts in front of me or do any more of that bad stuff around me, I'm going to tell my grandfather, so he can kill you."

"If you tell your grandfather, and he kills me, then he will go to jail, and you'll never see him again," he contemptuously replied.

I knew at that moment I had to be silent and protect my grandfather. The stakes for the truth had just gotten raised, and I was not going to get hurt or be without my grandfather. I perceived I had hurt him once before—when I told my grandmother about his lady friend at the ranch—and I wasn't going to do it again.

✳ ✳ ✳ ✳

As a girl, I learned to be quiet about the stories others told, even when they included me, because there could be punishment. The people I cared about might get hurt. As an adolescent, I learned not to speak about sexual acts perpetrated on me, because I was going to be questioned and made to feel wrong, and the people I cared about might be hurt. More and more experiences in life came to reinforce this conditioning of silence, more lying to myself, more losing sight of my truth, and more living my conditioning.

The questioning and silencing of my formative years would alter my natural progression into adulthood. As a grown woman, living in a big house with lots of nice things, I pretended everything was good. I accepted the relationship I was in and by doing so, I had to be silent, not tell my story, and be treated dismissively. The life I lived met familial and societal expectations coupled with my conditioning.

A little girl yearning for love and to be shown that she was special had now grown into a woman still yearning for love and to be cherished. Now, as an adult woman, showing my biological father around a house he expressed so much admiration for, I dismissed the urge to tell my story, what was really happening behind the doors of that exquisite home. I chose my conditioning, because I didn't know anything different.

I was living someone else's version of me until I began to excavate, reveal, accept, and love myself. It took me a long time before I could speak with my true voice. Now I've become a woman who is no longer silent, hidden, or confused, because I live in my Truth and Power. My amazing, resilient, and once-hidden mother, she too now speaks her truth and is no longer silent and lives in her power. We have changed some of the systemic conditioning we once allowed to dominate our lives. Little did I know, my entire life has been created to understand, discern, accept, and see the conditioned responses that once guided my life and other individuals. Now, fortified with knowledge and truth of the invincible power of woman, I coach women by teaching them how to have their heart desires while telling their stories, excavating conditioning, and learning their power.

What do you want?

A superlative relationship...

A fulfilling life...

Inner Peace...

To know your Truth...

To live your Power...

To know you matter...

By the end of this book, you'll know (when you choose) how to create and command the Life-of-Delight that you truly desire and deserve.

CHAPTER TWO

WHEN NOBODY
IS TALKING

Words are powerful. They carry emotional currency. They become what informs our thinking and serve as liberators or oppressors. I didn't learn the power of words until I began being oppressed by them, along with the beliefs within the communication and the conditioning, which followed those beliefs. Conditioning that had never been questioned or examined, yet "the words" were running my life. A beautiful parallel to the power of words is the effect of listening. Listening has a potency that cannot be compared to anything. It's the direct pathway to living a life of fulfillment. Attuned listening creates experiences of more joy and inner peace, which become a perpetual Way-of-Being. Our words are the source for fulfillment, truth, and power, or they can be used for dissatisfaction, unfulfillment, and deception; we get to choose.

I, like most human beings, want to know I matter, be able to express myself fully, and experience LOVE. Learning the potency of words and listening, my life moved from unexamined conditioned responses to a life of discernment and Self-Honoring Choices. I didn't know I was living my life as a result of conditioning until I was living a life that was unimaginable from any dream I had ever held for myself.

You don't have to wait until your life is in peril before choosing to learn about yourself and your conditioning. Are you willing to take a journey with me to discover more about yourself? Do you really want to get to know yourself?

Are you ready to be more discerning, make Self-Honoring Choices, and live a life that fulfills you?

✳ ✳ ✳ ✳

Once upon a time in my life, prior to discernment, I thought the act of a person, particularly a man, hearing me talk meant he was listening. I would accept the return communication as beneficial feedback, even if I didn't feel right about his response. I thought I was being heard, and therefore, I must matter. If a man gave me his seemingly undivided attention, I thought it was something of value.

✳ ✳ ✳ ✳

The first time I was consciously aware I was giving my power away was when I was in my early twenties. The choice I made didn't feel right, yet it was consistent with my conditioning and mindset.

The information that dictated the choice came from a man who was a leader in business. He managed a large corporation, had numerous employees, and he often gave me his undivided attention. I thought I mattered especially to him, because not only was he well respected and a business leader, he was my boyfriend. My obedience of listening to him, accepting his feedback, and doing what he said, even when I felt uneasy about it, provided a crucible moment and was the epitome of not trusting or valuing myself.

I met my boyfriend while in college and working part-time for a vibrant, stylish, and gorgeous woman in her late sixties. This woman was different than any woman I had encountered before. She wasn't afraid to say whatever she thought, and she did whatever she wanted. Not only was the way she acted different, the model of her lifestyle was something I had never been exposed to prior to meeting her. She was the person in charge. Her name was Madge. Madge also had a boyfriend who was her business partner and although she allowed him to give her counsel about business, she made the final decisions. I would witness her attorneys, bankers, accountants, all of whom were men, tell her what to do. She would consider their input, but she had the final word. I was in awe of Madge! In the beginning, I worked part-time, and after being with her a few months, she offered me a full-time salary while I was still working part-time, which included the responsibilities of being a general manager. She remarked, "You being here twenty hours a week allows me to manage my life more efficiently. You have great leadership skills." My relationship with her was beyond the parameters of employee/employer. I would have dinner with her and her family, we would run personal and business errands together, we shopped together, and sometimes, we had weekend cocktails. I enjoyed working and playing with Madge. Our relationship was heartfelt and unique, I felt very protective of her, and I understood I was an employee with lots of perks. Some of my responsibilities were writing checks for business expenses, overseeing the weekly budget report of how much money was spent from her "just in case" account, along with her personal and business accounts. Oftentimes, her personal and business expenses were commingled, and it was my responsibility to make her aware of the balances and overages, which I did forensically. When I thought anyone in the family or business was spending too much, I would have a conversation with them, and later, I'd inform her about the conversation. She was always quite pleased by my diligence and my ability to oversee, manage, and aid her with her finances.

Madge trusted me. I admired her. We had mutual regard, and I definitely knew I mattered to her.

One day while preparing to leave the office, Madge called and asked if I would come to her home and pick up the signed checks she had prepared for me. It was customary for her to give me a stack of blank and signed checks to disperse accordingly. So, when I left work, I went to her home, and when I arrived, she asked me to assist her with the last pieces of packing for her month-long holiday, which I did, of course.

After we completed the packing, she handed me a larger stack than usual of checks, walked me to the door, kissed me on the cheek, and said her usual mantra, "Make sure we always have what we need."

As she said those words, I thought, "I need to pay my tuition." Then I heard my *Inner Voice*: "Ask her. She'll help you." However, I didn't ask her, and I dismissed the thought. "Have a wonderful evening and a great flight in the morning," I said.

"I will call you from the airport," she responded.

And down the walkway I went.

On the drive home, the idea of asking her to assist me

with paying my tuition resurfaced in my mind. Working for her was fabulous in many ways, yet even with the increase in salary, it didn't pay enough for me to take care of all my new financial responsibilities. Soon, I was going to have to suspend my education or get loans, or a miracle needed to happen. When I arrived home, my boyfriend was there sitting in his car in the driveway. We had planned a date for that evening earlier that week, and I had been slowly building up the courage over the past several days to tell him of my financial situation and ask for guidance. I needed to tell him I could no longer afford going to college, because I was going from paying tuition at a state university to needing to pay tuition at a private university. My reluctance to tell him was that I didn't want him to think of me in any way other than a smart and self-supportive woman who had it all together. A point of reference I used for courage was reminding myself of one of the stories that Raymond had shared with me about his lean financial years when he, like me, was in his early twenties and going to college while working. Raymond often praised my dedication to balancing school and work so well. The more I reflected on our similarities regarding our college experiences, the more certain I felt confident about sharing my current financial struggle with him. Little did I know, that night would change me forever. The conversation we had soiled my personal integrity, belief system, and Inner Guidance. Prior to that evening, my younger brother had been the only male in my life whom I would share my highs and lows with. So, to share myself fully with this man and allow him to see me beneath the image he had of me was a huge leap, unfamiliar, and would later prove to be an insidious choice.

> Have you ever looked at someone through the eyes of adoration and respect, then experienced them as a person of compromise and disappointment?

As I got out of the car, I noticed a large and beautifully wrapped box in the front seat of his car. I got into the car and picked up the big, beautifully wrapped box. He said, "Don't open it yet. I want your excitement to build!"

I smiled. He took the box from my hand, put it in the back seat, and closed my door. He returned to the driver's seat and off we drove. We began driving down the hill from my house when I realized I had left the checks in my car. I asked Raymond to turn around. He didn't ask any questions. He simply went around the block, so I could get my "something" (the workbag) from the car. As we drove to the restaurant, I began laying the foundation for the conversation I wanted to have with him.

I said, "I need your advice on something really personal."

He replied, "I'll give you the best advice I can, and if I

don't know what to do, I probably know someone who does. I will do or give you anything."

With a smile on my face that went from ear to ear, I said, "Thank you."

In my mind, his response confirmed I mattered, which was of paramount importance because that reply made me more confident than ever that he would give me great counsel.

The drive to the restaurant was filled with conversation about our day and the possibilities of what could be in the beautifully wrapped box in the back seat. About five minutes before we arrived at the restaurant, he began a series of accolades. He communicated I was one of the smartest women he had ever met. He complimented my ability to balance my work and school life, and my commitment to my family; from his perspective, I could achieve anything I wanted. With every compliment, my confidence and the desire to tell him my story began to wane. Increasingly, I felt the need to hide and be quiet. I no longer wanted to tell my story for fear it wouldn't allow him to think of me as perfectly as he had just described me. We pulled up in front of the restaurant, the valet opened the door, and I got out of the car with my workbag in hand. I noticed Raymond give me a questionable look when I grabbed the bag.

Shortly after being seated at our table, we ordered two tequilas neat, oysters, and flatbread. After our cocktails, I developed liquid courage and decided I could share the financial situation I had mentally and emotionally been preparing to discuss with him. I began the conversation by sharing the trust I felt for him and the nervousness I had regarding communicating what I was about to say. *I didn't want to be judged differently than how he saw me.*

My vulnerability garnered the response of these words: "You can talk to me about anything, and I mean absolutely anything! I love you, and I am here for you!"

So, the conversation began, and I expressed my lack of financial preparedness for transferring from a state university to a private university. He listened to every word without interruption, and he held my hand through most of the conversation. In my mind, I felt this was another confirmation that I mattered and I was important to him.

After I finished speaking, the first words out of his mouth were, "I don't have any money to give to you, but I might know someone who does."

"Oh, no! I'm not asking you to give me money. I'm just asking for guidance. I need a plan. I don't know what to do, and I don't want to quit college. You told me about all the things you had to do when you were my age to earn money.

You said you went to people you respected, and one person gave you a plan. So, please, help me with a plan."

He replied, seemingly dismissive, while no longer holding my hand, "Yes, but my path was very different than yours. So let's enjoy the evening. You can open your gift now, and we can talk about this tomorrow. Is that OK with you?"

I reluctantly agreed by nodding my head in compliance.

He motioned for our server to bring the gift to the table and place it in front of me. When I opened the box, there was a smaller box with an envelope inside of it. The envelope contained a travel itinerary to Tahiti. I was completely surprised! The gift was an announcement that he was extending and including me in a business trip. All the reluctant feelings I had just experienced seconds earlier while nodding my head in compliance immediately diminished. I received this gift thinking it was one of the nicest things anyone had ever given to me, and with this mindset, I thought he would obviously aid in developing a plan that would remedy my financial transition.

Several weeks prior to that evening, Raymond had told me about his upcoming trip to Tahiti, and while he shared the details of the trip, I said, "I never thought about traveling to Tahiti. Perhaps I'll add it to my dream travel list."

He responded, "Perhaps I'll take you there one day and make your dream come true."

After opening the gift, the conversation for most of the evening revolved around Tahiti. Shortly before we left the restaurant, he said, "By the way, what's in your bag that's so important that we had to turn around and get it?"

I opened the bag and showed him what was inside and said, "They're from my boss. I picked them up right before meeting you. She regularly gives me a stack of signed blank checks to pay bills and make sure the office has whatever it needs." There was silence for a few seconds between us, and then I said, "Maybe I should ask her for guidance."

He responded, "Maybe."

He peered into the bag again, and this time, something felt wrong. I felt nauseous like I had to throw up, but I didn't say anything. He closed the bag with a curious look on his face and our conversation returned to talking about Tahiti.

He declared, "I'm going to give you the greatest experiences of your life while we're in Tahiti."

When we left the restaurant, the drive back felt awkward. Most of the ride was filled by silence. When we returned to my house, he pulled into the driveway, turned off the ignition, and said, "I think I might have a resolution for your situation."

"What is it?" I asked.

He replied, "You have the money you need. Write a check."

The moment he completed his sentence, I thought I was going to vomit. I knew what he was saying was wrong, and I thought, "How could he say that?" I was repulsed by his words, mentally and physically. Yet, I didn't get out of the car. I didn't say, "I never want to see you again!" I didn't say anything. I did what I was conditioned to do. I sat there, stayed silent, hid my feelings, and surrendered my power.

He continued the conversation by justifying the act of writing a check for myself. As he talked, everything within me told me to get out of the car and to get away from him. However, that's not what I did. I stayed in my seat and continued to listen. At the end of the conversation, he reached into my workbag, pulled out one of the checks and said, "She gives you these checks because she wants you to have everything you need, too." He said it with conviction! I wanted to believe him, that what he was saying was true. However, I knew writing a check without her permission wasn't the right thing to do.

> Have you ever known something is wrong? You feel it in
> every fiber of your body, and yet you allow yourself to
> be convinced otherwise.

As I went to bed that night, I could hear Raymond's voice saying, "She wants you to have everything you need, too. Just write yourself a check." The next morning, I woke up conflicted and wrote the check. Shortly after I wrote the check, I called Raymond and told him what I had done. He applauded me for taking action, told me how much I mattered to him, that anyone in my position would have written a check long before then, and I was doing what Madge would want me to do. With each word he said, I still knew he was wrong and I had become complicit. Yet, I convinced myself to believe him, because that was easier than admitting to myself what I had done and the poor choice I had made.

Later that day, after the conclusion of my classes, I went to work. When I arrived, I had the burning desire to tell one of the employees about what I had done. Instead of her condemning my actions as reprehensible, she agreed with Raymond. She told me that instead of lamenting for weeks over my financial situation, I should have written a check long before. She counseled me, "Never tell anyone. Balance the ledger and enjoy your new university."

By the end of the day, I decided to deposit the check and

never speak about it again. I was determined to enjoy transferring from a state university to a private university. As days passed, it was like I had never written the check and had almost forgotten about it completely.

That experience was not only about the choice of right and wrong. It was a commentary about growing up under the dominant conditioning that creates emotional and psychological quagmire. In my foundational years, I was punished for telling the truth when it diminished or compromised the image of our family. I was praised for lying or admitting the truth when it was favorable to the image being portrayed or being the girl following the man's lead. The lines between right and wrong were compromised and blurred based upon the circumstance. Yet, my Inner Knowing was constantly speaking to me. I chose to ignore it to succumb to my conditioning. And in this circumstance, Raymond said I was doing what was best.

However, instead of listening to my Inner Knowing and trusting myself, which was something I wasn't conditioned to do, I listened to my boyfriend. He was a man who was highly respected by his employees, friends, and the community. He was the same man who told me he loved me and I mattered to him, and who was taking me to Tahiti, and I wanted to trust him. So I allowed myself to believe him, because that was much easier, based upon my conditioning, rather than thinking I could steal.

When have you compromised your personal integrity
or made a choice that wasn't self-honoring based on
your conditioning or wanting acceptance from a man or
another?

Writing that check to myself was the first time I was consciously aware that there was an *Inner Guidance* directing
me. From the moment Raymond told me to write the
check, my *Inner Guidance* was telling me the opposite.

Are you aware of your Inner Guidance? Do you listen and
respond as directed?

Few people knew of my dishonesty, yet I always carried the
regret of not asking Madge prior to writing the check and
not disclosing what I had done after writing the check. The
other part of this was the shame I carried for being dishon-
est, hurting Madge and not trusting nor honoring myself.
Shortly after Madge returned from her trip, I quit my job
and ended the relationship with Raymond. Although I
didn't think about my self-betrayal, there was something
within me that felt amiss and detached from others. In
conjunction, I began feeling disdain for Raymond, and I
didn't want to be around Madge anymore. I didn't know it
at the time, but it was this incident that began the deeper
erosion of regard for myself. Meaning I was willing to let
others inform, guide, and direct my thinking and actions
and not trust myself. Over time, I would move to such

a distance from myself that physically, mentally, and emotionally, I would end up somewhere unimaginable.

There I was, almost twenty years later, living in a big, beautiful house located in an affluent suburb in Texas. I owned lots of adult toys, yet, with my live-together boyfriend, I was facing another life-defining decision. This time I was listening to my *Inner Guidance*. I was different, although I didn't know it until my only choices were self-honor or complete self-demise. Words were no longer my oppressor. The conditioning of male dominance was almost completely extinguished. This choice was going to be wholly mine and the moment I made the choice, everything in my life would change.

* * * *

His name was Gordon, and I moved halfway across the country for him. The plan was that we would marry, start a family, and build a business. We wanted to contribute to humanity by providing beneficial services that would create more of an equal economic playing field. The dream was we would be the family that would create a legacy that would last for generations. That was the dream and the plan, and yet, our reality was something completely different.

* * * *

It was early Thursday morning. The house was acutely quiet.

"You're not doing it right! Can you just do it right?" Gordon said in a demeaning and forceful tone.

His complaint quickly escalated to yelling and then ranting of my incompetence to properly bandage his finger. This wasn't anything unusual at that point in our relationship. Numerous times before, I had watched his personality go from gentle and sweet to insulting, and then he would become a monster within seconds.

"Hurry up! I have to go!" he snarled.

And without a reply, I did exactly as he commanded.

After I finished bandaging his finger, he said, "You're nothing! You're less than nothing! You better be glad I love you and that I'm going to marry you, because no one else would."

As I said, it wasn't the first time I had watched him turn into a monster; however, this time I had enough. I never thought in a thousand years, actually in a million years, that I would be a woman who would be in a relationship allowing a man to speak to me in that manner. As the words came out of his mouth, this time I knew I was leaving him. I wasn't coming back, and this relationship was over. In a nanosecond, I felt a surge of power, and I was no longer afraid of anything. In the past, I was fearful to leave him, scared of what others may think of me, and I was terrified to be alone. I felt uncomfortable by making such a strong stance and by breaking patterns of my conditioning.

Within a couple minutes after I'd bandaged his finger, he left the house. He slammed the door so hard when he left, I could hear it from the second floor. Once he was in the carport, I heard him get into the car, then out of the car, and before I knew it, he was storming up the back stairs. He ran into the house like someone was chasing him. He came into the bathroom where I was cleaning up from changing his bandage. He resumed ranting, this time about the timeliness of changing his bandage.

He said, "If you had changed my bandages more quickly, and you weren't so slow, then I wouldn't have gotten upset. I don't understand what takes you so long." He paused and then said, while staring at me so intently it was as if he was looking through me, "Are you afraid of me?"

I didn't respond. I just looked at him with a blank stare on my face.

"I have to go now. We'll finish this conversation when I get back home. You know, I am really sick of you making me act this way! And you better be home when I come home from the office." He left in a huff and sped away in his car.

I was so pleased when he left the house. Actually, I was more than pleased every time he left the house. About four months prior this rant, I had already begun sleeping with a hammer under my bed just in case I had to protect myself. I was having recurring visions of Gordon shooting me while I was in the shower. I also had visions of him choking me while I was sleeping. Enough was enough! It was beyond time for me to leave him. Once upon a time, I'd left him and returned. This time I was leaving. I knew it was over, and I was never coming back.

Every material thing I owned was in that house. The dream of who I thought I should be was represented by that house, and the vision for a family and my commitment to everything I thought I should be for him all lived in that house. And, as of that day, I knew I was ready to leave it all and walk away. I didn't know where I was going or who I could call for support. I just knew I had to leave. I was more than 1,500 miles away from my family and friends. I was alone *but not really alone.*

I went through my mental Rolodex of people I could call locally, and with each consideration, I knew not to call them because of their relationship with Gordon. I knew they would judge me harshly. I suspected many women, like me, who had what I had, materially, were also living in darkness and shame. The moment arrived when I knew it was time to pack my clothes and get out of there. And I couldn't even remember where I had stored the luggage. I felt frenzied, panicked, lost, and in danger. I had no one to call, nowhere to go, and I was leaving. As I stood at the front door looking at the downpour of rain with my body chilled to the bone, it occurred to me to call Carla Davidson. Carla is a mother, grandmother, great-grandmother, and a successful businesswoman. She is a woman of prayer and faith. She was probably the most unlikely person for me to call, yet I was guided to call her. And this time, when my *Inner Guidance* spoke to me, I listened and responded accordingly.

When she answered the phone, I didn't even say hello. I was trembling so badly, I could barely get the words out of my mouth. I said, "I need to come to your house. I have to leave Gordon."

Within twenty minutes, she was at the front door, and without any questions, she recommended that I follow her to her house.

Gordon had recently given me a 560SL Mercedes. It was one of the many gifts given to me to prove his commitment and love. According to Gordon and my father, men only make sizable financial contributions through gifts and monetary expressions when they really love a woman and are committed to her for the rest of their life. Whether I wanted the gift he purchased or didn't want it, if he wanted me to have it, he purchased it anyway and would declare it was his outward demonstration of the love he felt for me. The car, like the house, was something I wanted, yet I didn't want them given to me based upon the so-called proclamation of his love for me. His love meant he had complete control of me. The purchase of the car was an attempt to have me stay when I was preparing to leave him months earlier. When he brought it home, he said, "I know this is your dream car. I'm going to make all of your dreams come true, and each time you drive this car, you'll be reminded of how much I love you."

I didn't want to follow Carla to her house in that car; however, there was no other option. Driving the car wasn't a reminder of how much Gordon loved me. It was a reminder of how much I wasn't honoring myself.

Before leaving, I wrote a note that said, "I don't want to be here. Don't call me. I will call you tomorrow. This relationship is over! I will no longer take your violence as anything other than what it is, detrimental to my life."

I placed the note on the refrigerator. I walked through the kitchen door, down the back steps to the carport, got in the car, and waited for Carla to drive around the back and meet me. As she pulled up, I noticed her car was filled with boxes, bags, and all sorts of things.

She rolled down her window as did I and said, "When you called, I heard the urgency in your voice; I was headed to the donation center, but I figured I had to come here and not go there. That's why you need to drive yourself. You're going to follow me. I will drive very slow, and I want you to know everything is going to be OK."

We gave each other a smile of acknowledgment as we rolled up our windows, and I followed Carla to her home.

When we arrived at her home, she escorted me to the study. I sat on the couch and began talking, and to my surprise, I told her the entire story of my relationship with Gordon. By the time we concluded our conversation, my eyes were red and swollen, nose running, and two boxes of Kleenex had been emptied.

> Have you ever given yourself away to another or lost yourself so completely that as you recount the story, you are almost unrecognizable to yourself? Have you ever asked yourself, "How did I get here?" or "How was I ever there?"

In a soft, caring voice, Carla said, "I could tell by the way he studied you and was always watching every move you made that he wanted control of every aspect of your life. You are too powerful to be with a man like that. Actually, no one should be with a man like that. He's an abuser, and it's obvious he believes he possesses every aspect of you. A man like him would rather kill you than allow you to be free. And you are a free spirit." I listened intently while still sobbing. Every word Carla was saying, I knew was true, and I wondered if she saw it, could others see it too? She continued, "Sweetheart, killing isn't always by physical death. It's most often an emotional and psychological death; men like him will strip away all of your beauty, both inner and outer. I'm glad you had the courage to leave."

The next day, I called Gordon and reiterated what was written on the note. He calmly said without pause, "I'm sorry for the way I acted yesterday. I need you to forgive me, and I custom ordered the dining room set you wanted and it's coming tomorrow. It's going to be a temporary set. Your permanent dining room set takes eight weeks to make, and then they will ship it. See how I do everything to make you happy? I'm making them bring you a temporary dining room set tomorrow. Everything I do is for you. What time will you be home?"

It was as if Gordon hadn't heard a word I'd said, nor did he believe the note I had left on the refrigerator. I said firmly, "Our relationship is over!" without acknowledgment of anything he said regarding the dining room set or accepting his apology.

He calmly replied, "You aren't leaving me. You can't leave me. So stop playing games and come home."

"You're not listening, and I'm going to hang up!" I said.

He responded this time in a forceful and harsh tone, "Be home when I return this evening, and I'll forgive you for even thinking you can leave me."

Then he hung up the phone abruptly. I sat there holding the phone, stunned by his remarks. I decided in that moment I needed to go back to the house and pack all my things. I knew he would be leaving the house shortly, and I would have a full day to pack. Carla recommended I go to the house and pick up just a few things and not try to pack all my things until I had a more solid plan.

I called a friend, Dana. Carla called her assistant, and the four of us went to the house to pack my things in preparation for having them shipped to California. It had been less than twenty-four hours since I was in that house, and yet when I walked through the front door I felt an overwhelming sense of anxiety. It became difficult for me to breathe. My head was spinning, and I thought I might pass out. By the time I went upstairs, my symptoms were exacerbated, and I think I had a panic attack. The girls did their best to calm me down. And I reminded myself this was my exit. I would never be here again, and I was safe.

We sorted clothes as best we could, the things Gordon had purchased for me from the clothes I moved to Texas with. My breathing continued to become more labored. I felt increasingly nauseous, and I knew it was time for me to get out of that house. No matter how much I tried to calm myself, I just wanted to flee. I left the house while Carla, her assistant, and Dana stayed and continued packing. Everything Gordon had purchased for me, they nicely folded and put in the guest bedroom upstairs. And everything that was mine prior to Gordon, they packed in boxes, taped, and put near the front door.

When Gordon returned that evening, he found my clothes boxed for shipping and a letter on the refrigerator saying, "IT'S REALLY OVER! I will conclude all the business affairs that I usually take care of for the last time. Meaning I will pay all the household bills, business accounts, and all outstanding bills due from vendors. Please know I will be purchasing an airline ticket so I can return to California. Please ship my clothes to my mother's home address. Everything you have purchased for me is in the upstairs guest bedroom, and you can do whatever you like with it. I have the car and will return it as soon as I can."

I didn't hear anything from Gordon that evening. However, when I awoke, there were several messages from him, ranging from expressions of sorrow and being apologetic to anger and retribution. One of his messages said, "Nobody leaves me! You're not leaving me! You need to change your mind and get your ass home!"

Well, I didn't change my mind. I didn't go back to that house. It was never a home. I never saw Gordon again, yet it wasn't over between us.

When Carla allowed me into her home, and I shared the details of our relationship, I never felt judged by her; I only felt her acceptance. I became aware shortly after having that conversation with her that I didn't have to judge myself. I realized that all my self-imposed judgments were opportunities for me to learn more about me. Leaving Gordon taught me I had courage and that deep down I love myself and could trust myself; being in a relationship with Gordon was not loving. Leaving him defied my relatedness and conditioning regarding men. Actually, I was revealing my innate Self by releasing my conditioning and listening to my *Inner Guidance*. Leaving him, I was being born anew.

As I learned to stop judging myself, I also learned to forgive myself. I had to forgive myself for getting into a relationship with Gordon. I had to forgive myself for not listening to my *Inner Guidance* from the first date and through the relationship. I had to forgive myself for not making Self-Honoring Choices. I had lots to forgive. Then came reconciliation. I had to reconcile with myself what happened in that relationship and how I got there. It took years to reconcile within myself all that I had hidden and ignored about me. Remember, no matter where you are in your journey in life, self-acceptance and examining familial and societal conditioning are paramount to truly knowing yourself.

I had been living in Carla's house for about two weeks. The plan was to close out my life in Texas and return to California. Most days during those two weeks I was unable to focus on the business at hand. I barely ate, and stayed in bed for days. It was about eight in the morning on Sunday when Carla began knocking on the bedroom door and asking, "May I come in, please?" She opened the door with a big smile on her face and said, "I think it's time for you to join me at church, leave this room, and get out of the bed."

I accepted the invitation and joined Carla, her daughter, and grandchildren for church. The service was especially emotional for me. Meaning throughout most of the service, I was crying. There was a heaviness that occupied my mind and body. Minutes before the conclusion of the service, the minister invited anyone who wanted extra prayer to come to the altar. I definitely needed extra prayer, so I went to the altar. One by one, the minister stood in front of each person, put his hand on their forehead, gave a blessing, and whispered something in their ear. Then, one by one, each person returned to their seat. When it was my turn, the minister put his hand on my forehead, gave me a blessing, and the next thing I remember I was opening my eyes while on the floor with warm tears streaming. The entire congregation was gone except for Carla, her family, and the ministerial team. After about five minutes or so of lying on the floor with my eyes open, I felt steady enough to stand up. There was one person on my right, another on my left, and someone at my head. On the count of three, they each aided me to a standing position. Then one of them escorted me to a chair. As I sat there, I reflected upon what had happened. When the minister put his hand on my head and began praying, I began talking to God. I heard, "It was for the evolution of your soul." As I sat in that chair, I felt different. I no longer felt the heaviness, the burden, or haunted by the experiences I had endured with Gordon or any other experience that I deemed as bad. I felt empty, victorious, and peaceful. Yes, I was different.

✳ ✳ ✳ ✳

On an almost daily basis, I experience women living marginal lives because they've chosen to hide themselves. Although most often their choice isn't a conscious one, it's a by-product of their conditioning. The outcome is the same—women living marginal lives. Each time a woman chooses not to tell her story, accepts vulgar language as defining language, and chooses to suppress her desires for the benefit of appearances, then words are her oppressor, and she is living a marginal life.

When a woman looks at the life she is living with a clear heart and assesses where she is in her life related to the choices she's made of self-honor versus conditioned responses, then words are her liberator. Please choose to break the cycles of conditioning that don't serve you or us, and move into the paradigm of living a fulfilling life. That life includes making Self-Honoring Choices, peacefulness, and being a Mother-to-Another. A magnificent woman came to my aid in a time of need. She gave me exactly what was required. She gave me what I refer to as "a mother's love." Carla gave me what we can all give to one another...mothering when needed. It's imperative for you to learn who you are independently of your conditioning and to fully accept yourself.

CHAPTER THREE

ASKING QUESTIONS

Have you ever asked yourself these questions?

- Where and how did I learn to relate to men?
- Who taught me about men?
- What do I think a man will bring to my life?

If you've asked yourself any of those questions, I applaud you. If you haven't asked those questions, perhaps you've asked these:

- Where is my man?
- How come I'm not experiencing the love and connection I want with a man?
- Am I being myself or someone else's idea of me?

If you haven't asked yourself those questions, that too is completely OK.

Most of my life, I didn't even know there were questions to be asked about my relatedness to men or myself. The questions posed earlier became evident as I began to make Self-Honoring Choices. If you're ready, ask yourself the questions posed earlier, and whatever the answer (I mean the first thought that comes forth), that's the contribution to your whole answer, and you're on the pathway to understand more about yourself. From my life experiences, those questions were formulated, and with each question and relationship, I was able to define what I wanted to feel, what I required emotionally, and how I wanted to be treated, and it gave me clues about my individual magnificence. I've used every relationship with a male counterpart as an integral part of my learning. It has led me to know and understand I am the Prize...you are the Prize...we are the Prize...every woman is the Prize. While learning and gaining understanding that I am the Prize, I also had to learn about cherishing and honoring myself. I came to the understanding it was necessary for me to know the Truth about myself through honoring and cherishing myself before I could have the expectation that someone else could do that for me. Do you know that each relationship is relevant? It's because when you look closely, as I did, you will see with each experience there is something for you to learn about yourself. Through learning, wisdom is planted and conditioning starts being dismantled, if you allow it. So I invite you, as you are moving into learning more about yourself, not to discount any relationship you've ever had or any relationship you are currently involved in. Use every relationship for your learning and allow it to catapult you into wisdom. Then watch what begins happening in your life.

When examining my previous relationships, I recognized the comparable characteristics between the men I dated and the men who influenced the formative years of my development. Without a doubt, the patterns modeled were learned in childhood and expressed throughout my life until I learned differently.

> Men have all the power, and a woman's role is to seek their guidance, take their direction, and make them happy. That was part of my learning and conditioning.

Relationships created as adults are built upon the learnings and observations from childhood. The patterns of behavior, when unexamined, continue throughout our lifetime until we decide to excavate our conditioning, learn who we truly are, and choose how we want to live. It's only when we examine our conditioning and become aware of our unique magnificence that we can claim our life as our own.

> The seeding from my grandfather, biological father, and bonus father informed me that men have all the fun, control, power, and are the leaders. Everything commenced around making them happy and doing whatever they wanted personally to fulfill their needs. In addition to supporting them in their business affairs, the woman's role was to be polite, pretty, an informational source, make everything look good, and never speak ill regarding any man.

I gravitated to and identified with the men in our family. I emulated their behavior as much as I could. I, like the men in my family, expected the women in our family to serve my needs. I saw myself as one of the guys. Actually, I saw myself as my grandfather (he was the first man in my life), and he was the best guy among all of the guys, from my perspective. He was the first man in my life I called "Daddy." Somewhere between middle school and high school, I began calling him "Grandpa," because I called my biological and bonus father "Daddy," too. I didn't want to call my grandfather the same name I called them.

As a child, I saw my grandfather as the man of all men. He was always dressed in a way that made me think he was so cool, and when he had on a suit, it was perfectly fitted with a handkerchief folded nicely in his jacket pocket. His shirt, tie, socks, and shoes were always coordinated. My grandmother made sure of that. She was like his personal valet when it came to his wardrobe. When he was in casual attire, he would wear cotton pants, a white T-shirt, and a short-sleeved button-down shirt that complemented the color of his pants. For bed, he wore pajama pants and white T-shirts. When he would go fishing or hunting, he had complete outfits that mimicked those from the sporting magazines that were around the house. He always wore cologne and made certain he smelled and looked good before he left the house, no matter what his style was for the day. He was a man who was always concerned about his physical appearance. So of course, he always had a fresh haircut, nails manicured, and hair dyed, when necessary. He was proud of his worldly accomplishments and his family. He was generous to everyone around, and he was the purveyor of fun. He was a dominant force in our family and seemingly the director of everyone's actions. He navigated the lives of our immediate and extended family. He really enjoyed his life and lived according to his rules. He was never concerned what others thought of him. He was only concerned with what he thought of himself. Grandpa's nickname for me was "Mama." And although he was a man of few compliments, family and friends would tell me things he would say about me like, "You're his heart. The sun rises and sets on you. You're the apple of his eye." I believed what others told me because Grandpa made me feel special. He most often treated me like the sun rose and set on me; we spent lots of time together.

When he was around, I got everything I wanted, and everyone treated me especially nice. He was my favorite person. When I was in college, Grandpa began cooking Sunday brunch for my brother and me, and sometimes it included the whole family. Eventually, it morphed into Grandpa making brunch for a host of longtime girlfriends and me. We would sit around the kitchen table for hours talking, drinking, and eating. Grandpa listened to whatever we wanted to talk about, and what we wanted to talk about mostly was boys. Brunch wasn't complete until Grandpa would tell a story about the unscrupulous behaviors of men. One of the lessons he would often make reference to was "giving the milk for free and not buying the cow." During one of our brunches, my friend Farley shared her excitement about a man she was dating. She also shared that she thought this might be the man of her dreams and told Grandpa, "When he proposes, you're going to be the second person I call after my sister." Grandpa listened and never made a comment until she asked him to.

"Do you want the truth, or do you want me to make you feel good?" he replied.

"Both!" she responded.

Grandpa didn't give her the truth. Instead, he made her feel good. He later told me the truth. He said, "Farley is too excited about that man, and she can't see what's going on in front of her. Mama, I just didn't want to hurt her feelings. If a woman gives herself to a man for free, she's foolish! And milk just isn't sex; it's your time and your energy," he said.

I somewhat understood what he was saying. I wanted an explanation, and I didn't ask. Looking over the landscape of my life, I became aware it was during those brunches I could recognize my inability and conditioning to never question a man. Also during those brunches, I became aware of the questions that I wanted to ask my grandfather directly related to the rumors I'd heard while growing up. Interestingly, I got enough courage to ask questions about his life, yet I wouldn't ask him questions that might have contradicted or demeaned what he was saying. Following are some of my courageous questions:

"Did you help your brothers and sisters when they relocated to California by assisting them in purchasing their first homes and getting jobs?"

He responded, "Yes. I made lots of money, spent lots of money, and gave even more money away. Mama, a good man always does whatever he can do to support his family."

Next question: "Did you help my bonus father begin a business?"

"Yes. I helped him start a business. He was working for a

company, not satisfied; he reminded me of my younger self, and I wanted to make sure he could provide lavishly for your mom, your brother, and you. A man wants to be the leader in his life, and in order to do so, he has to own his own business, so he can be in charge of his income," he replied.

Next question: "Did my biological father work for you?"

His answer: "Yes. When he was in high school, a senior, I gave him two things: a very nice car to drive that he would return every evening and pick up each morning, and the principles of entrepreneurship, which included him working for me, so he could learn firsthand what a business owner does. Mama, a man is always in charge of the money. He has to know how to make it, so he can then bring it home to his family. Men need to be taught from a young age how to earn money."

I appreciated my grandfather's willingness to answer my questions.

In retrospect, I recognize the questions I asked were those that validated him and made him even more notable for me and my friends. All my close friends knew my grandfather, and they too called him Grandpa because he was the purveyor of fun. As I said earlier, he was the man of all men and, from my perspective and that of my close girlfriends, he was an all-around great guy.

These are the questions I never asked my grandfather:

"Why did you punish me as a child for telling the truth?"

"Why did you stop taking me to the ranch with you?"

"Why did you have intimate relationships with other women?"

If I had asked these questions, I would have been going completely against my conditioning and the way I was taught to relate to men.

From child to woman, my grandfather was a constant influencer in my life. He was the first person that mattered to me who said, "You talk too much." It was also within the dynamic of my relationship with him that I learned of punitive consequences for telling the truth. He was the man who always looked out for me, protected me, and made sure I had whatever I needed. He demonstrated through those brunches that I mattered to him. However, the seeding in my formative years that he contributed had to be examined and excavated so I could have a fulfilling life.

One day, when leaving brunch, Grandpa said, "Mama, you're about as sweet and pretty as any girl could be, and you remind me of my favorite girl on television. You're a good girl, Mama. You're the best girl ever." And with his million-dollar smile he bent down, kissed me on my cheek and said softly, "Thank you, Mama." I noticed he had tears in his eyes. It was the first time I had ever seen him with tears. Pretending as if I didn't notice them, I returned a kiss on his cheek, squeezed his hand, and said, "See you next Sunday, Daddy."

I am grateful for those brunches with Grandpa. I wish he was still alive, so I could get to know him better, ask him questions from the paradigm of knowing I'm the Prize and making Self-Honoring Choices. I'd also like to ask him who taught him about his relatedness to women. When I began examining my conditioning, the relationship with my grandfather gave me the opportunity to look at his life with neutrality, learn through his choices, and gain wisdom from the outcome of those choices. Ultimately, my grandfather aided me in defining what I wanted and needed, and what wasn't acceptable from a man.

The next man in my life was my "bonus father." He was a constant in my life from about the age of two. I called him Daddy or Dad when he asked me to and, like my grandfather, everything revolved around him, at least for the most part. His mood dictated the entire household. I didn't know from one day to the next what his interactions would be regarding me. He was consistently inconsistent; he was nice and then mean towards me. He exposed me to new things like different areas of the city, architecture, nationalities, food, restaurants, and neighborhoods and gave me a perspective of the world. That's when he was being nice. Then he would abolish or discourage me from things that he perceived girls didn't need to do, like sports, being curious, and learning more; that was his conditioning regarding women. When I would be punished for no reason, had my favorite things taken away, and when I had to wash dishes that were already cleaned, yet according to him were not clean enough, that's when he was being mean to me. The state of our relationship was never consistent or peaceful until shortly before he passed away. Our relationship reflected his inability to wholly despise or love me. Right before he passed away, I believe he made the choice to love me, because he apologized for the way he treated me while I was growing up. I don't believe he was a bad person. I think he was a product of his upbringing, conditioning, and social understanding. I'm certain he was the best father he knew how to be to me and gave me the best he knew how to give. Today, I am grateful he was my bonus father.

The third man in my life is my "biological father." I have few memories of him as a child. It's impossible for me to give commentary of his treatment towards me as I was growing up, because he was absent. So it was his absence that I learned the most from. The dynamic of our relationship, for as long as I can recall, has been one of getting to know each other. We have many of the same habits. We see certain areas in life through the same prism, and our ideologies for humanity are similar. My biological father is a man who definitely identifies a woman's role is to support and do whatever her man needs to be done for him and the family. And the man always comes first. Over the course of us getting to know one another, he is beginning to understand what a woman of Power looks like. I am a woman and a daughter who is different than my father's ideology. In many ways, I'm an enigma to him because I don't fit into his understanding of a woman... however, he is learning who I am and what female self-honor looks like. I'm certain he loves me, and we are still getting to know each other.

My grandfather, bonus father, and biological father reinforced the same conditioning in various ways. The overarching communication by word and deeds was: it's OK to be haphazardly treated.

I know many of us have had the pendulum of treatment that swings from seemingly good to seemingly bad, and the experiences have come through our caregivers, parents, and those present in our formative years. If you're willing to begin examining your relationships and bridge the similarities between those who seeded you in your formative years and the men you dated, you'll be surprised by the discoveries. Remember, use every relationship for your learning, and allow your learnings to become your wisdom.

LDW are the initials of the man I have loved since the first time I saw him. Prior to my husband, he was my greatest cheerleader. He has seen me in seemingly good times and during the times when life looked dark. I have always known he loves me and that I matter to him even when he was emotionally distant. He showed me love before I knew how to love myself fully. He is my brother, and his steadfast love, devotion, and regard for me was contributory for defining what was possible in a man and some of what I desired from and by a man.

CHOOSE A MODEL OF LOVE

As you excavate yourself and are discovering the similarities of conditioning with relatedness to men, especially the men you've dated, I also invite you to *choose a model of love* that you want to experience.

> Think of one person who has shown you consistent love or imagine what consistent love would feel like. Then write on a piece of paper one quality and one action that you would like to see in your romantic relationship as well as whatever quality you'd like to experience in that relationship. Embrace that quality for yourself right now as well as whatever action you would like to see.

EXAMPLE:

Quality = Tenderness

Action = Heartfelt Communication

Result = When having a disagreement, you can be mindful of your words and know that you love one another. The communication clearly shows tenderness and kindness are some of the pillars of the relationship, and the disagreement is simply discourse.

In the past, my conditioning allowed my life to be divisive. Meaning I was split within myself, and the nurturing I received didn't allow me to fully express or examine me. As a child, I had the reinforcement that communicated I am special, I am nothing. I watched the women in my environment live from the paradigm that men are superior, and I mimicked the behavior. For decades, my life reflected my conditioning. I too treated myself as if I were special at times and as if I were nothing at other times. In other words, I treated myself haphazardly, and I allowed others to do the same. By taking the time to release *systemic conditioning and patterns*, I now have a Life-of-Delight! If you're willing, you can do the same by releasing that which binds you, allow yourself to think differently, get to know the real you, and move into a conscious life of Self-Honoring Choices.

CHAPTER FOUR

OUR BODY, OUR LEARNING

My sexual education was succinct, incomplete, and yet I received more information than my mother was given when she was blossoming into womanhood. The nuns at school informed me I only needed to touch my vagina to clean it. There was no need to look at it, and if I looked at it or touched it other than for cleaning, I would be committing a sin and punished. My mother's male gynecologist educated me at our first appointment, which she scheduled a few days after I began my first menstruation, by telling me I could get pregnant. He told me to mark on the calendar the first day and the last day of each menstrual cycle, and he instructed me to clean myself in my private area especially during my menstruation. Education continued by my aunt saying, "Whenever you have questions about sex, I'm here for you to ask." And the last staple of sex education came in a large box, which arrived approximately a week after the appointment with my mom's gynecologist. The box contained menstrual pads, cotton panties, and a pamphlet that explained how to use the pads. Also included was an informational story telling me I was no longer a girl, I now had menses, I was considered a woman, and I could get pregnant. I told my best girlfriend at school when the box came and what was in it. I shared with her all the information that was written in the pamphlet. I thought every girl got a box like mine when her period began. So what I thought I was doing was sharing with Polly what she could expect when her box arrived. I soon found out, after telling Polly, who told someone and that someone told another about the information I shared with Polly, that I was the most informed girl in our junior high about our menstrual cycles.

It's necessary to educate ourselves about our whole self, which includes our bodies and sexuality. Whole-self acceptance contributes to our ability to make Self-Honoring Choices and to create a fulfilling life.

The information I learned as a girl I shared with my peers. Recently, one of my childhood girlfriends reminded me that I taught her how to use and dispose of her menstrual pads, in addition to teaching her how to calendar her cycle. She said I made her not afraid of what was happening to her body, and prior to me, no one except the nuns at our school had ever talked to her about her body. As girls, we can learn and teach others how to become a Mother-to-Another by sharing information.

When I arrived at college, I thought I was ahead of the information curve regarding my body and sexuality. Since I had heard nothing different from junior high through high school, I still thought I was the most informed girl. When I was in my first sexuality class, I think the name of the course was Our Anatomy and Sexuality, we were assigned to sit or stand in front of a mirror and look at our bodies, then instructed to take a small handheld mirror, put it between our legs, and look at our vagina uninterrupted for about ten minutes. Our professor remarked, "This will be one of the shortest homework assignments you'll ever be given by me." My assignment took what seemed like forever to complete. I was horrified by the assignment! I wanted to do my homework. I attempted to do my homework. Yet with each attempt, I felt like I was doing something wrong, bad, and I was going to be punished.

✳ ✳ ✳ ✳

The absence of having a relationship with our body compounds the need to be silent, hidden, and not wholly engaged with Self. Without Whole-Self Awareness, we can never learn how to embrace ourselves fully. Learning to wholly accept myself was inclusive of developing a nurturing and loving relationship with my body. I'm grateful that I stand in my feminine power now, and I live my sexuality in this wondrous female body. Today, I understand the sensuality of womanhood, and my vagina and I have become BFFs—best friends forever.

How would you describe the relationship you have with your body?

Does it feel nurturing and supportive to your femininity and sexuality?

Do you use your body primarily as a sexual magnet?

Are you disconnected and see your body only for functionality?

Whatever your answers are, remind yourself there is much to reveal about You. When you begin to uncoil the cord of your conditioning and begin truly learning who you are, then miraculous discoveries will happen.

❋ ❋ ❋ ❋

Conditioning and patterns run our life until we excavate and examine them.

My first date was when I was fifteen and a half years old. It was a double date with my best friend, Amy Grimes, and her boyfriend Oscar. My date was Oscar's friend Paul, who had a crush on me. Amy and I were so excited about our first dates. We purchased matching outfits, got manicures for the first time, and we went to a professional hairstylist. We felt all grown-up and wanted to look especially pretty. Amy and I both learned in our formative conditioning to always look pretty for "your man." Although we were only girls and they were boys, we were already mimicking the adult roles of our conditioning.

The boys arrived on time at Amy's house as planned. Mr. Grimes stood at the front door as the boys walked up the walkway and the four steps, and onto the porch to the front door. Amy and I weren't allowed to greet them at the door when they arrived; that was Mr. Grimes's job. Mr. Grimes invited them into the house, escorted them into the living room, and then he pulled the pocket doors closed. The doors were closed for about twenty-five minutes, and when they opened, Mr. Grimes invited Amy and me to join them in the living room. The boys stood up as Amy and I sat down. Mr. Grimes instructed the guys to give us the rules for the evening. Oscar started with rule number one, "Be gentlemen at all times." Then Paul gave rule number two, "We're leaving as a foursome and stay as a foursome throughout the date," and so on until number fifteen. We had fifteen rules to follow, including being home by 10:30 p.m. Well, we did it. We complied with the rules, returned to Amy's by 10:30, and we had the best first dates ever! By the end of the date, which included hamburgers, French fries, go-kart riding, and almost climbing a tree, I too had a serious crush on Paul. The four of us continued double dating for dates two, three, and four. On our third date, Paul and I had our first real kiss, and while kissing, he touched my breast. Yuck! I didn't want him to touch my breasts, and once he did, I didn't know what to do because I wanted him to continue to like me. When we finished kissing, I was kinda happy about our first kiss, yet I felt shameful because he touched my breast.

It was Saturday, and we were going to Disneyland for date number four. I really wanted to go to Disneyland, and I didn't want to see Paul because I thought he might want to touch my breast again. I told Amy what had happened, and she said, "It's OK for him to touch your breasts as long as you have your clothes on. It's really, really OK."

The guys arrived at noon with a flower for each of us, a bag of chocolate kisses, and two packs of gum. The moment I saw Paul, I felt especially nervous, shameful again, and I really didn't want to go. I almost said, "I'm not going." Yet, I said nothing, and off we went to Disneyland.

Surprisingly, the date was going along perfectly, my nervousness and shame dissipated, and I was enjoying myself. While at the amusement park, Paul and I held hands, exchanged small kisses, and rode lots of rides. On the drive home from Disneyland, we stopped at the miniature golf course we had seen from the freeway on our way to Disneyland. The stop wasn't part of the original plan; at least it wasn't part of my plan. Apparently, at some point while at the amusement park, it was decided (unbeknownst to me) to divide into couples and have separate private couple time. In my mind, this translated that Paul was going to touch my breast again. As we drove into the parking lot of the miniature golf course, I felt nauseous, and although I didn't think I was going to throw up, I certainly pretended as if I might vomit.

When Oscar parked the car, I jumped out quickly with my hand over my mouth. I looked for the sign to direct me to the women's restroom. When I located the restroom, I frantically ran into a stall and stayed there several minutes while trying to figure out what to say to Amy, Paul, and Oscar. I couldn't tell them the truth. I wanted Amy to still be my best friend. I wanted Paul to like me and not touch my breast. I wanted Oscar to think I was a nice girl, and I didn't want to have private couple time. That was my truth, and I didn't think I could say any of it.

After several minutes, I came out of the stall, and there

she was, my friend Amy. Amy said, "Maybe this wasn't a good idea and we should go home?" I extended my hand to her. She placed her hand in mine, and we walked hand in hand to the car. When we got back to the car, the boys asked if I was OK. I said, "I don't feel well. I think we should go home. I might throw up."

Well, I didn't feel like I was going to throw up. What I felt was nausea because I didn't want Paul to touch my breasts again. Everyone agreed we should go home, and that's what we did. We got back on the freeway and went home.

Paul called many times after that date, and each time he made it very clear he was disappointed I got sick. He told me he wanted to touch my breasts, and he was hoping I would pull up my shirt and show him my breasts. He also said it looked like I had very pretty breasts, but he couldn't be certain until he saw them.

Remember, relationships are formed by the seeding in our formative years until excavated and examined.

✳ ✳ ✳ ✳

Post excavation:

Antonio wasn't celibate, although he was taking a break from sex for awhile. In one of our many conversations about sex and my choice to be celibate, we gave ourselves clear boundaries and rules. The rule was to always communicate honestly. The boundaries: no touching Mr. Penis or Ms. Vagina. Both the agreement and the boundaries were mutually agreed to. In the midst of our first kiss, Antonio paused and asked, "Are you ready to end your celibacy?"

I chuckled and replied, "No."

"I think it would be something special for both of us if you ended your celibacy today," he said.

"I'm not ready to give myself to you in that manner," I answered.

He didn't respond, and the kissing continued with the same boundary as it began. I didn't know it at the time, but I was building the muscle of self-trust and learning more about loving myself. I was making clear and definite choices about my body. I was communicating those choices, and Antonio was respecting my choices. I was becoming the woman I wanted to be, a woman whose life is governed by Self-Honoring Choices and an unwavering dedication to Self.

We talked the entire drive back to my house about our kissing constraint and my commitment to celibacy. As I exited the car, I found myself liking Antonio even more because, instead of trying to pressure me to have sex, he respected my choice, he wanted understanding, and he agreed.

I said, "We need to keep sex out of our relationship until we're definite we want to be in a long-term relationship with one another. I don't want my heart to be broken, and I don't want to hurt you."

Almost a week passed before we saw one another again. The plan was that I would meet him at the bistro where we had our first date, and then we would go to the home of Jim and Jackie to have dinner, just the four of us. When I pulled into the valet at the bistro, Antonio was already waiting for me in his car. From the moment I got into his car, he was nonstop talking. He was more complimentary than usual and seemed overly excited about our evening. He remarked many times, "This is going to be a great evening for you!"

When we arrived at the home of Jim and Jackie, where we were having dinner, he quickly parked, got out of the car, opened the door for me, took my hand, and guided me into his arms. It was like a scene in a romantic movie. We began kissing, and unlike the kiss a week prior, I felt a deep connection with him. I thought while kissing, "He may be the one."

Then it all changed when he tried to move my hand to his penis. I redirected his hand, and this time, he tried to force my hand to his penis. I stopped the kiss and asked, "What are you doing?"

"I'm giving you what you really want," he replied.

"I get to decide what I really want, and you putting my hand on your penis isn't what I want. What's gotten into you?" I inquired.

"Nothing's gotten into me. It's time for me to get into you," he declared.

I was shocked! It was as if I was having a conversation with someone other than Antonio.

"Take me back to my car!" I exclaimed.

With a firm and loud tone, he said, "I think you're overreacting."

I repeated, "I want you to take me to my car NOW!"

After several minutes of him trying to convince me to go into the house, he again said, "Please calm down. I was giving you what I thought you wanted, and don't embarrass me in front of my friends."

And then, with no audible words from my mouth, I said, without speaking, "Take me back to my car now!"

He read my lips and said again, "Calm down!"

It was very curious that he kept telling me to calm down when I was completely calm. I wasn't enraged, angered, or hysterical. I was definite, unwavering, and ready to go back to my car.

When we returned to my car, he pulled behind it, and he didn't get out to open the door for me. I said firmly yet sweetly, "If you open the door, we may go out again. If you don't open it, there isn't a chance for any further communication between us."

After about a minute, he got out of the car, walked to my side, opened the door, and extended his hand.

I didn't talk to Antonio for a couple of days after that experience. We met at the same bistro for lunch the following week. He apologized profusely. I was negatively surprised by Antonio's behavior on our previous date, and I was in awe of the Self-Honoring Choices I made for myself. While sitting at lunch in the bistro with Antonio, I felt more powerful, and I recognized that my choices on the previous date affirmed, to me, I was loving myself in a different way. At the end of our lunch date, I thanked Antonio for the fun we shared and told him I no longer wanted to see him. This was a monumental stance for me, because in that moment when I chose to tell him I didn't want to see him anymore, what I was really saying, in addition to the obvious, was I know without a doubt I matter. I have a voice, I don't have to hide, I get to choose what I want and how I want to be treated, and I'm declaring to make choices that honor me. Wow!

※ ※ ※ ※

Prior to examining my familial and societal conditioning, I thought money, houses, clothes, jewelry, cars, and travel were the most important contents for a happy and fulfilling life.

> Are you willing to take dominion over your thoughts and actions and no longer respond to life from unexamined conditioning?

I was silent until I learned my value. Once I learned to speak up and began telling my story, little by little I experienced more courage, fortitude, and self-love. Every woman deserves to be free from the conditioning that informs us to be silent, hide, and accept circumstances as they are and beliefs that our most substantive value is our body. It is time for all of us to tell our stories and live in our unique and magnificent power. It's time to release the illusion that external things provide ultimate happiness. It's time to create a Life-of-Delight by making Self-Honoring Choices, by being a Mother-to-Another, and absolutely experiencing whole-self acceptance. Let's be powerful together! Life is so sweet when excavated and examined!

Are you willing to excavate and examine yet?

CHAPTER FIVE

CREATING A LIFE-OF-DELIGHT

I experienced sexual trauma as a child, was in a so-called domestically abusive relationship as a woman, and I learned from both of them. I've experienced various lifestyles. I know how to live in the paradigm of superficiality, affluence, and influence. I've existed with two dollars to my name, had multiple thousands of dollars in my bank account, was conditioned to be silent, hidden, and without inner peace, and I learned from it all. My life has ranged to both sides of life's spectrum and much of the middle. Today, I am filled with self-knowledge and wisdom. I have chosen to be an advocate for every woman who is willing to let their light shine, know themselves fully, and honor themselves by examining their conditioning.

> I am loving, wholly accepting of myself, and share love unconditionally with the world.

It's an understatement to say that once upon a time "wholly accepting myself" was a notion so far from my comprehension it didn't have any existence in my reality. Once I began seeing and living from the paradigm of whole-self acceptance, I learned the intrinsic, magnificent beauty of me. Now, what was once beyond my comprehension is my reality. When you know yourself, inner peace comes and resides within you, and then comes the attunement of your magnificence. You will begin to define situations and experiences accurately once you excavate, examine, and attune. Your life will reveal something new—deriving from Truth, not conditioning. You will use the whole of your life as your curriculum, and will learn from it all. Over time, you will become the person you've always wanted to be—the person of your dreams.

Sexual violence, trauma, rape, and so-called domestic and emotional abuse are all among the most heinous acts, mostly committed against women.

Why is it when a woman or girl has one of those atrocities committed against her that she is often marginalized by being held in some way responsible for the act committed against her?

Why is the act minimized and the woman left emotionally, psychologically, and sometimes physically fragmented?

Why do we women protect and defend the men who violate us?

When I consider the evidence of rape; sexual, domestic, and emotional abuse; violence; and trauma, I am convinced these are among the most villainous psychological and physical acts perpetrated against humanity. Each of these societal atrocities interrupts the patterns of emotional congruency and oftentimes leaves emotional and physical scars that can take a lifetime to mend. Let's take a look at the definitions and the outcome of some of these villainous acts that are committed against many of us.

RAPE

The definition according to the dictionary reads: "To force a person to submit unwillingly to sexual intercourse."

An accurate definition of rape is: the culmination of brutality, violence, trauma, and control. It's a savage violation of an individual's mind, body, and spirit.

ABUSE

The definition according to the dictionary reads: "Abuse is defined as misuse, addressed rudely."

Sexual abuse: Ironically, it isn't even collectively defined. Sexual abuse is another indication of the minimization of the act. So let's define the words individually.

SEXUAL

The definition according to the dictionary reads: "Sexual is the adjective derived from the word sex, which is defined as sexual intercourse, the act of procreation in which a male penis is entered in a female vagina."

An accurate definition of sexual abuse, defined collectively, not singularly: When a person or persons of dominance misuses their position or influence to damage, traumatize, and/or destroy that innate sacredness of one's sexual integrity by brutalizing the psyche and physicality of another.

Domestic abuse is also defined as two words according to the dictionary.

DOMESTIC

The definition according to the dictionary reads: "Domestic is defined as in the home, home loving of animals kept by man in his own country. Tame. Accustomed to life. Adapts to its environment."

The words "domestic" and "abuse," from my perspective, are unrelated to the definition of the occurrence. There is no way that domestication lends itself to the psychological and physical torment of that experience.

An accurate description of so-called domestic abuse is: When an individual undermines and erodes, through manipulation, their partner's value and uses violence of any sort, which includes words and deeds to control the behavior of their partner. It distorts reality, and life becomes a daily practice of survival, and peace of mind is absent.

You get to accurately define your experiences and nothing is marginal.

You get to tell your story void of blame, shame, or regret.

* * * *

One of my childhood girlfriends was especially smart and beautiful. She lived in one of the most prominent homes in our neighborhood, and had an older brother and two younger sisters. Her parents were very involved at our school and spent a lot of time with her and her siblings. The family would go on two holidays per year, and one of them was always out of the country. I wanted to be her sister. Carrie had what I thought was the perfect family. I would often go to Carrie's house to do homework, play jacks, and just hang out. I spent as much time as I could in their home. I was frequently invited to stay for dinner, which always made me happy, because I enjoyed feeling and pretending as if I were part of her family.

After having dinner in their home numerous times, it occurred to me that Carrie and her older brother never sat next to each other, nor did they ever talk to one another. Once I made this observation, it became obvious they were avoiding one another. Something wasn't right between them. I never asked what was going on, and I think the reason I didn't was twofold; firstly, because I didn't want to disrupt my perception of being part of the perfect family, and secondly, I didn't want to put Carrie in the position to say something bad about her brother (because after all, although he was a boy, in my perception, he was a man). Years later, I learned the truth of what was happening in the pristine home with the seemingly perfect family.

Carrie and I remained close friends until we graduated

from high school. Then we lost touch for more than seventeen years. We reconnected at the wedding of another high school friend. Seeing Carrie at the wedding felt seamless, as if no time had passed between us. We exchanged contact information and began communicating somewhat frequently. It was about a year after our reconnect that we had the conversation about her brother. The conversation was surprising, not shocking.

Carrie recounted stories of her brother fondling, kissing, and eventually penetrating her. Her first memory of intercourse was when she was six years old. Carrie eventually told her parents, who cried as she told them her story. They apologized to her for what had happened, and then told her to never tell anyone that story. Carrie was heartbroken and stunned, and felt betrayed by the two people she thought she could most depend upon. Her parents sent her brother away for about two months. During that time while her brother was absent from their home, she attempted to have further conversations with her mom and dad about what had happened. With each approach to her parents, she was silenced and told, "We don't talk about this anymore."

Carrie was forced to suppress her words, which followed the suppression of her appetite and led to extreme weight loss and other related health issues. Her parents became extremely concerned by her physical appearance and her inability to eat, which led them to seek therapy for Carrie. After a couple of private sessions with Carrie, the therapist enrolled the parents in their weekly sessions with them. In a small office decorated with degrees and other notable successes on the wall, Carrie wept as she recounted part of her story to the therapist. She omitted all parts of the story that had anything to do with sexual abuse, trauma, or violence. Carrie noticed on the therapist's wall one of the degrees was from her father's alma mater, and Carrie didn't want to embarrass her father. After Carrie concluded telling this very watered-down version of her story, her parents gave their opinions on what could be causing her eating problems. Yet, they never mentioned the sexual abuse or violence she had experienced. After a couple of sessions with her parents, Carrie recounted she couldn't take it any longer and exploded. She told the therapist everything, absolutely everything she had experienced from her brother as well as her parents' omission of the truth and their decision to never speak of it again after she confided in them. *Carrie had honored their request up until that moment.*

She said, "I thought I was going to die when I told the therapist. Then I realized I was already dead. The day my parents asked me to be silent, something inside of me died, and each day, I felt less alive."

Shortly thereafter, the whole family began therapy. Carrie

said, "Therapy was extremely difficult, and it emotionally distanced me from everyone in my family. However, after time, I began to see myself, and for the first time in my life, I got to see me, and not the image of me I was living. This was the most truthful I had ever been with myself."

When Carrie graduated from high school, she got as far away from her family as she could. She hid herself from me and from everyone with whom she'd had a relationship during childhood.

She said, "Therapy helped me see clear enough that I needed to get away from all the lies I had been telling myself, all the lies I allowed my family to tell me, and the illusion I was living. My parents made me believe I was safe, supported, accepted, and could tell the truth always. None of that was true."

So many women are silenced and are not able to tell their story. However, we can evolve beyond our conditioning, move into our Truth, and begin to live powerfully.

Excavate, learn, release conditioning, tell your story, and move into the paradigm of whole-self acceptance because **YOU really matter**. Remember, through revealing, accepting, and understanding who you are, your life becomes powerful. It is imperative for every girl and woman to know they matter, and share their unique magnificence. It is incumbent upon all of us to give definitions of accuracy to what is happening or has happened in our lives. We must tell our stories and free ourselves from any oppression that came from conditioning.

...YOU really matter!

Your Real Truth Is Your Power!

CHAPTER SIX

THE FIRST MEN IN MY LIFE

I had four serious relationships that I could look to for information that would allow me to discern the value and lack thereof I held for myself when I began excavating. Serious relationships, meaning we dated more than a year, our communication expressed we were dating with the idea of marriage, and we had independent relationships with the other's family. I'm thankful I didn't marry one of those men. I am grateful for all I learned, and I am awestruck that each of them mirrored, in some manner, the modeling of the conditioning "It's OK to be haphazardly treated." Remember, relationships as adults are seeded from childhood conditioning until you excavate, examine, and choose differently.

Serious Guy Number One—"*My Intuition Was Sup-*

pressed." In college, my roommate and I were the first to have an apartment away from the dorm. Having an apartment made me feel completely grown-up. My boyfriend went to college across town and lived in a dorm with another student athlete. We would usually see each other once during the week, and we would spend some of our weekends together at our apartment or his mother's home. I didn't have a car yet, so when we stayed at his mom's, he would drive across town, pick me up, and then drive back across town so we could share time with his family.

It had been almost three weeks since we had seen one another due to his training schedule and classes. I was so looking forward to sharing time with him and his family that weekend! I had missed him. It was Saturday morning. The intercom rang from downstairs, and I buzzed him into the building, opened the door, and waited for him to walk down the hallway. There he came with a huge smile and a ginormous backpack that he carried almost everywhere with him. I think he had every book from every class in that backpack. He was a star athlete and an outstanding student. I held the door open as he crossed the threshold, put down his backpack, and bent down to kiss me. He was more than a foot taller than me. The moment his lips touched mine, I knew he had kissed someone else. Instantly, tears began to roll down my face. I felt something within me disconnect. The kiss, intuitive knowing, tears, and disconnection seemed to happen simultaneously.

Without a pause from thought, I said, "Leave."

He wasn't even all the way in the apartment yet and I repeated myself, "Leave. Pick up your backpack and go."

He wouldn't go. Instead, he stayed for more than an hour trying to convince me my intuition was wrong, and he professed his faithfulness and love to me. I was unrelenting in my request for him to leave. Finally, he left, and I cried for the remainder of the morning because I was devastated he had kissed someone else. Up until that moment, it never occurred to me that there was a possibility he would kiss someone else. It wasn't even a thought. Through my tears, I told myself our relationship was over, and I would never see him again. Then I saw his backpack and knew I would see him one more time to return it.

Early that afternoon, his mother called. He got on the phone with her, and both of them told me I was wrong. His mother said, "He didn't kiss another girl. You're his only girlfriend. Perhaps you're feeling especially sensitive since you guys haven't seen each other for a while."

His mother continued to talk, saying things to remind me that from her view and his, we were a couple and a family.

"He loves you. He wants you to be his wife. He would never cheat on you. He would never kiss another girl. I didn't raise him that way, and you know that!" she stated. Later that day, he came back to pick up his backpack and me.

It was almost two semesters later when what I knew the day he crossed the threshold was confirmed. I went to his dorm between his training to drop off a bag of his favorite snacks. When I opened the door, there he was sitting on the couch wearing only shorts, playing a video game, and there she was, sitting at the study table wearing a bra and panties.

I was dismissive of the Still Small Voice and my Inner Knowing.

Serious Guy Number Two—"*I Was the Other Woman.*" Admiring friends and colleagues surrounded him. He was a leader socially and professionally. He enjoyed traveling, entertaining, and having new experiences. I thought I was valuable to him judging by the amount of time he spent with me and how he commanded others to treat me. Besides that, he said yes to all my requests. I chose to believe everything he told me even when it didn't feel right. He once told me to write a check from an account other than my own to assist with my tuition (and you know the story). I knew it was wrong, and I convinced myself to write the check anyway. When we met, he told me he was recently divorced. Then the story changed that he was legally separated. After dating for more than a year and wearing a diamond ring on my right hand, I found out I wasn't a girlfriend wearing a pre-engagement ring. I was a mistress wearing a ring given to me by another woman's husband. After learning I was a mistress, not a girlfriend who was soon to be his fiancée, I ended the relationship.

It was about a month after I ended the relationship when I finally had the stomach to meet him to hear his explanation. He said, "I wanted to tell you everything, but it was complicated, and I didn't want to lose you. I figured I could work out things with her before you found out." Before I could respond, I heard a female voice behind me say, "I'm never divorcing him, and you can have him." I turned around and his wife was pulling out the third chair from the table. I was shocked, scared, and speechless. By her communication and his behavior, it was obvious they planned that she would join us. She said, "You can have him without me, and he'll be broke, or you can have him with me and keep having fun. It doesn't matter to me. I just want you to know that I'm not going anywhere without getting what I deserve, and that's a whole lot of money that he's never going to part with just to be with you." She talked for more than twenty minutes without pause. By the end of the conversation, I concluded he was right, and she was wrong. He and I could have a dynamic relationship independent of her. I didn't care about his money, and I deemed she was of no consequence to us.

Nothing I told myself was the truth. Approximately two weeks after the encounter at the restaurant, I called Kim, his wife, and said, "I don't want him without you, and I don't want him with you. I'm very sorry for having a relationship with your husband. I had no idea he was married."

She replied, "There's no need for you to apologize. You couldn't have known that's part of our arrangement."

We talked for more than an hour, and during that time, I made her right, made him wrong, and felt sorry for both of them. From my perspective, they were ruining one another's lives and staying together only for money. As we were concluding the conversation, she said, "I can understand why he loves you. You're really special, and under different circumstances, I would want us to be close friends." Kim and I spoke two more times after that conversation. Each time she called, it was when she felt like she needed a sister friend. I concurred with her thinking; under other circumstances, we could have become very good friends.

Serious Guy Number Three—"*Family Ties*." From the moment I gave him my number, he was persistent to schedule a first date. During that time, my life was filled with family, friends, work, and exploring my spirituality. I felt as if I needed more than twenty-four hours in a day; my plate was very full. After about three weeks from the date I had given him my phone number, he left the funniest voicemail ever, which prompted me to call him back immediately. We scheduled our first date. Oh, my goodness! The first date was planned to perfection! Each communication prior to our first date, he'd ask questions about my preferences. I wasn't aware he was taking notes and planning to use each of my answers to craft a perfect first date. He said, "It took so long to get a first date, I needed to impress you, because I knew from the moment I met you, we needed a second date."

He picked me up from the art opening of a dear friend and took me to a restaurant that was usually booked for months in advance. We sat at a table with an ocean view and talked for so long that what started out as brunch was moving into dinner. At the end of our first date he said, "I might have to ask you to be my girlfriend if you're really this sweet." I don't remember if it was our second or third date when he said, "Whomever you're going out with, get rid of them because I want you to be my girlfriend, my fiancée, and then my wife. Will you please get rid of any other guys you're seeing, and will you be my girlfriend?" I said yes to both and looked forward to being girlfriend, fiancée, and wife.

The beginning of our relationship was magical. We were inseparable, minus working. He formed relationships independent of me with all of my family members, and I did the same with his. We would regularly meet with our immediate families, siblings, and parents. His family lived on the East Coast, and we would often travel to share time with them, and on some of those trips, my parents would join us. With each trip, I would meet more family and friends, and I became more involved in his family and community. His parents would also come to visit us on the West Coast. Each time they came, they too would meet other members of my family and they became part of our community. We mingled with family and friends in a manner that communicated we would inevitably be married. Then the unimaginable happened. A mutual friend told me my guy was having a relationship with another woman. I wouldn't believe it. I couldn't believe it. Then she gave me evidence. I confronted him, and eventually he confessed. I was crushed by his betrayal. We had a commitment, he and I; it extended beyond us to our families, friends, and others. All the dreams we shared and agreed we would live had ended.

Serious Guy Number Four—"*Knocked Me to My Knees.*" It had been about three years since dating Guy Number Three when I met Guy Number Four. The first time I had dinner with him, I knew he wasn't the man for me, and yet I made the choice to have a second date with him. Quickly, our dating moved into a committed relationship. He was the kind of man who needed a woman to make him feel complete, and I wanted a man who wouldn't be unfaithful.

I met him while he was on a business trip in California. To

be in a committed relationship with him, I had to move to Texas. He wasn't willing to date long distance, and I allowed him to convince me to do a three-month trial of living in his state before deciding if I would be willing to permanently relocate. Well, I did the three-month trial and didn't return to California until the relationship was over. Everything in this relationship was orchestrated by him for me to lose any identity I had before he came into my life. He gave me a nickname, and at first, I thought it was cute. It made me feel special. He said it sweetly, and he demanded everyone call me the name he had given me. I later found out he gave me a new name because he didn't want to call me the same name any man had ever called me before. The relationship ended when I was no longer willing to erase all of me, submit to his domination, and live as a prisoner.

Serious Guys One, Two, Three, and Four and other experiences in my life were the culmination and out-picturing from the seeding in my formative years. Until I excavated what was unknowingly conditioned within me, I merely existed and reacted to life occurrences based upon familial and societal conditioning. Today, I have new learnings and a different Way-of-Being, which constantly reinforces and mirrors; I am cherished, I matter, my voice is of contribution, I make Self-Honoring Choices, I am guided by my Inner Knowing, and whole-self acceptance is the model of my life.

Through the wisdom from excavation, understanding

my value, and the commitment to make Self-Honoring Choices, I have met, dated, and married the perfect man for me. His consistent behavior of kindness, loving actions towards me, and his unwavering commitment to his words are in alignment with who I've become. His life reflects values, morality, confidence, and kindness. I get to live in a perpetual state of loving, and life seemingly gets better every day (although each day seems perfect)! My life at this moment is directly correlated to learning to excavate, examine, acknowledge, and understand my once-lived conditioning. Learning *you* is the gift that perpetually gives. Your life becomes a daily miracle. You are the Prize!

Learning the value of yourself is absolutely the best and most precious gift you can ever give to yourself. I invite you to take the time to learn yourself. If I did it, you can do it. If you're willing to learn your value, be open to the possibility you're the Prize, your life will change in ways that are currently unimaginable. When you know you're the Prize, standards and qualifications are part of the blueprint of creating the life you desire and deserve.

Are you willing?

Are you ready?

This is your time!

Relationships as adults are the by-product of familial and societal conditioning until you excavate, examine, learn, and choose to make Self-Honoring Choices.

PART II

THE FULL STORY

CHAPTER SEVEN

MY CASTLE, MY KING, THE ILLUSION

I'm told by friends and have seen in the movies that first love usually happens in high school or college. That isn't my story. My first experience of romantic love occurred in my thirties. He was *Serious Guy Number Three*, Peter Gates. He was the man I thought I would marry, have children with, explore the world, watch our children marry, be grandparents, and leave splendid footprints of integrity for others to follow as a legacy. I definitely thought Peter was my prince. He was well educated, had a great career, attractive, and personable.

On our fourth date, he asked, "If I could do anything for you, what would it be?"

What came to mind was immediate, and it surprised me,

"I would like my parents to be friends instead of just being polite and tolerating each other," I responded. My reply and his fulfillment of the reply quickened my affection towards him. Within a matter of months, he orchestrated the reunion of my biological parents. They didn't just become friends, they too became a couple for the second time. Watching them rekindle their first love was a heart-fulfilling experience.

"I will always give you whatever you want. Plus, when we have children, we need their grandparents to be role models for marriage and happily married too," Peter said.

Seeing my parents happily together and being in a relationship where I felt cherished and adored was a first-time experience, and it made me feel purposeful.

Peter and I acted like high-school kids. We would talk on the phone throughout the day and in the evening when we weren't together. When we were together, he would take pictures of us and make mini-movies about our relationship. He displayed tremendous adoration for our relationship and shared it with others by making copies of our mini-movies and giving them to family and friends. He would often remark, "We will have these movies to show our children. Then we will create more movies with our kids and share those with our grandkids. We are creating a family."

From the time I was about twenty-one years old, I knew I wanted to create memories and experiences for my family that would surpass my lifetime, and with Peter, I thought our mini-movies were the beginning of the fulfillment of that dream. He listened to my dreams, and like my grandfather, he believed I could do whatever I said I could. Peter was the first man with whom I could envision everything we talked about becoming our/my reality.

One night we were having wine and cheese in the backyard, surrounded by candlelight and listening to music when suddenly I had the urge to tell him something that I held in shame. "I think we should tell one another our biggest secrets," I said.

"OK! You go first," he responded quickly.

I smiled, nodded yes, and thought I was going to speak, but the words weren't ready to come out of my mouth They were choked down by shame. All of a sudden, I felt so shameful about my secret that the words wouldn't come out. I paused, took a deep breath, and he said, "Whatever you want to tell me you can. It stays with me, and it's OK, whatever it is. You can tell me anything." Another pause, silence, and now I was ready to tell my story. I shared the secret of stealing from my employer by writing an unauthorized check to assist with paying my college tuition. It had been more than two decades, and in some ways, it felt like it was yesterday and a lifetime ago. Yet, I was still carrying the guilt and shame of that experience. I shared with him every detail regarding my possession of the blank signed checks, the encouragement of my former boyfriend, and the lies I told myself to excuse the actions. I told him everything, including how I felt like an albatross of shame was around my neck. I felt guilty, shameful, and disappointed with myself for never apologizing face-to-face and for writing the check. I also shared with Peter that although I had paid her back in full, I knew writing that check destroyed the wonderful relationship Madge and I had. As I concluded telling the story, for the first time since writing that check, I was able to fully breathe. I wasn't aware, until that very moment, of the gravity of shame I was holding onto. Miraculously, the albatross of shame had released its grip on me. I was happy and relieved to tell the whole truth and not be punished. I learned from that singular experience the power of speaking the truth to another. If you have an albatross of shame gripping you at this moment, I encourage you to find a person with whom you can be truthful, not have any punitive backlash, and tell your story. If there is no one with whom you have that level of trust, then go to the mirror and speak your story out loud to yourself. The power of speaking the truth is a path to Self-Honoring Choices. You don't have to hold shame about your life experiences because all of your life is the curriculum for learning. When we live in shame, it keeps us small, and oftentimes it makes us invisible. Shame keeps us from our power. So, be shameful about nothing and allow seeming mistakes or poor choices to be part of your character development. Let it serve as your life curriculum.

Peter encouraged me to keep talking and continuously reminded me I had nothing to hide. When I was complete with my sharing and had no more secrets to tell nor shame to release, Peter began telling his secrets. Over the course of that evening, we told our secrets and also talked about situations in our families, current and past, that we were committed not to repeat in our lifetime.

In our conversation, I said, "I think one of the worst things a man can do is cheat or betray a woman's trust in any way."

His reply, "That's nothing you ever have to worry about. I wouldn't ever break your heart. I would never betray you in any way. I think men who cheat are cowards, and there is no coward in me, Baby."

His words kissed my heart, and I melted into a cocoon of safety. I believed I could trust him completely, and we would marry one day and live all our dreams. Before that evening, Peter and I had spent lots of time together and communicated throughout the day. However, I still had many other areas of interest and other focuses that kept me occupied. After our conversation that evening, my attention became even more narrowed, and I began viewing life exclusively through the prisms of him and us. Telling him my secrets, in my mind, confirmed he was The One. Peter Gates was going to be my husband. I had found my prince and he was charming.

* * * *

It was early morning. The sun had yet to rise. The long stretch limousine was in front of the house and soon we would be heading to the airport. I wanted this trip to be filled with memorable experiences from beginning to end, so I reserved a pristine, well-stocked limousine with an attendant and driver to deliver us to the airport. It was over-the-top, and it was very exciting! This was going to be the trip that we would talk about for the rest of our lives. We drank mimosas, ate fruit, and had yummy freshly baked pastries while being driven. This was the first time my parents and I traveled together, and it was the first time I traveled with a man and my parents together.

* * * *

When we arrived at the airport, we had celebrity treatment, meaning everything was done for us. We even had one of those electric cars take us to the gate. Each of us was experiencing one WOW moment after another. From being picked up at home to the time we were ready to get on the plane and depart, it was awesome! When we arrived in New York, Peter took the reins from there. He planned our arrival and trip in New York with a similar mindset as I'd planned our departure from California. The rental car was awaiting us. The hotel had us all on the same floor, but at opposite ends, and the restaurant he selected for the first meeting of our parents was perfect. I had taken care of planning details on the West Coast, and he had taken care of the plans on the East Coast. For me, these were more signs confirming he was The One and we were good partners.

We arrived at our hotel having two hours to unpack, relax, and prepare for dinner. When my parents entered their room, they surprisingly found a note from Peter's parents saying, "Welcome to our Family!" and in our room, there was a note that read, "We have a daughter!" I was more than thrilled by the kindness expressed, and in my mind, it was yet another confirmation I would marry Peter.

My parents, Peter, and I arrived at the restaurant and waited in the lounge area for our table to be ready and for the arrival of Peter's parents. From the moment his parents, Helen and John, arrived and were introduced to my parents, there was an instant connection among them. It was as if they were longtime friends. When the maître d' came to apologize for keeping us waiting for our table, none of us were aware it was past our reservation time, because everyone was engaged and having a delightful time! Instead of moving to a table, we decided to have dinner in the lounge area. During that evening, it was as if we were playing musical chairs because we took turns sitting with one another until each of us had the opportunity to have a one-on-one conversation. By the conclusion of dinner, it was obvious to each of us that something very special was happening among all of us. Over the next three days, my family and I were introduced to other members of the Gates family, friends, coworkers of Helen and John, plus Peter's childhood friends. The entire trip was a blast! It was beyond what I could have dreamed of, and it was exactly what I wanted—memorable experiences from beginning to end. When we returned to California, Peter made a mini-movie of our trip and sent copies to almost everyone we shared time with while in New York. For weeks after the trip, I would receive cards, calls, and emails saying things like, *"Welcome to the family! So happy to meet you! Your parents are terrific! Looking forward to the wedding! You'll be great parents! You're a great couple!"* There were so many lovely expressions of kindness.

In my mind, each was an affirmation that one day Peter and I would get engaged, be married, have children, eventually be grandparents, and grow old together. Our story was supposed to be "happily ever after." I believed all of those things would happen. Although we had no date scheduled to marry and no scheduled plans, we just talked about all those things. And we talked about them often.

"One day we will be married." I didn't know it then, and it took me a long time to learn that I was living on *Fantasy Island*. At my core, I didn't have the value of me yet. Therefore, there was no way he could value me enough to move our conversation to a plan and execute it for me to be his wife. I believed, like so many women, in the words of a man and behaved accordingly. I assumed his actions would follow. What I learned was...

> Action is execution. Action makes it happen, and words are the possibilities of what can happen when action is applied.

One day Peter asked, "Who would be the bridesmaids in our wedding?"

As I was answering the question, I stopped and said, "Why do you keep acting as if we're planning our wedding, and you haven't proposed? This is becoming all fantasy conversation."

My tone was harsh, and it was a completely different tone than I had ever spoken to Peter in the past. Earlier that day, I had received a call from Peter's cousin. In our conversation, she told me a story about a friend of hers who had been strung along for years by her boyfriend, who eventually left her after he got his dream job. I'm certain the conversation I had with Peter's cousin prompted the heated tone of my conversation with Peter.

He responded, "We always talk about our marriage. I'm preparing everything for you, because when I marry you, I need to be able to take care of you for the rest of our lives. I have to do things in a logical way to make certain I'm able to give you everything you want. I really want you to have everything you want. Do you understand what I'm saying?" He was beaming with happiness. I could feel his heart through his smile. I happily nodded my head in agreement. My takeaway from that conversation was everything was for my benefit.

* * * *

When a man tells you he can't put a promise or engagement ring on your finger, because of whatever reason, I caution you to examine his words and actions. Then use your discernment to know if what he's saying is a stall tactic or a necessary choice that is moving you in the direction of marriage. When I surveyed men who are happily married, one of the common denominators was that they each proposed marriage or offered some type of talisman to communicate their intent for marriage as they did whatever was necessary to secure the future with their wife.

* * * *

Peter had given me words and introduced me to his family and friends, and I allowed that to be enough to communicate I was his intended wife.

It had been months since our family trip to New York and the holiday season was approaching. Peter and I decided to combine our families for Thanksgiving dinner. After talking it over with our parents, it was confirmed we would celebrate Thanksgiving in California. Dinner was going to be at my place, and we planned for it to be a feast! Peter, my mother, my aunt, and I cooked Thanksgiving dinner. We cooked for days, and by the time dinner was ready to be served, we were all exhausted yet very pleased with how well everything turned out. It was a wonderful experience preparing and sharing Thanksgiving dinner as one big happy family! For me, this was another confirmation that one day Peter and I would be husband and wife.

Helen and John enjoyed Thanksgiving dinner and spending time with my family. As a matter of fact, they enjoyed it so much that instead of leaving two days after Thanksgiving as scheduled, they stayed for six more days. During their stay, we scheduled two dinners with the sole purpose of having conversations about our families' future, marriage, children, and where we would live. Yes, we were going to have a conversation about marriage with our parents, and yet we were not engaged. In our second dinner, Peter expressed his dream of purchasing a large home in a historic community not far from his parents, refurbishing it, and making it our dream home that we could pass down to our children and keep in our family for generations.

He said, "I want to live in that community all the days of our life together." He talked about raising our kids, having festive Thanksgiving dinners each year, building a grandparents' suite, and creating family traditions. He painted a picture of the life he wanted to live, and as he talked I thought, "This is my dream life!" Peter was detailing the life I desired. I had shared my dreams with Peter before, yet I wasn't aware during the conversations he was truly listening to every dream (just like he had done in preparation for our first date). I shared, and he incorporated all my life dreams into his life vision. As he communicated his dreams for us with our parents, I became more committed to him, meaning not only was my focus narrowed on him, but my conversation would turn to "we" instead of "me." I believed wholeheartedly, without question, we would only be parted by death, and we were in a real partnership. I believed this by his words, no actions, and without him asking me to be his wife, without being engaged, I was committed...completely committed.

By July, we were in escrow for our "dream property" on the East Coast and still not engaged. The property was everything Peter and I had dreamed of, plus more. The house had a basement that could be converted into a theatre, there was an area for the gym, step-down living room, grand great room, spiral entry staircase, and it had already been completely refurbished. The seller of the property was a female real estate developer who had restored the house for herself and her family. Her circumstances changed, and she and her family were no longer going to move in. With her expertise, architectural sophistication, passion for development, and the thought that this was her home, she had given every attention to detail. This home was masterfully restored, and it was an exquisite property. The first time I met the seller, she shared the dreams she had for her family in that home as well as why she was selling the property. Her story touched my heart, and it also explained why she made the acquisition especially easy for us.

Her story was she and her husband had two children, planned to have two more children once they moved into the new house, and they would live in that home the rest of their lives and leave it to their children. Her dream was reminiscent of the dream Peter and I shared. While telling her story, she shared that her husband had always wanted a piano although he didn't play. For his birthday, she was planning to give him a piano and piano lessons. She said, "I wanted him to have everything he wanted in our home because he taught me how to dream and had made most of my dreams come true." Her life changed as well as the life of her children one afternoon when driving to an appointment to look at a piano from a private seller. She saw her husband's car pulling into the valet of a luxurious hotel. She said, "If it had been a regular day, I wouldn't have thought anything about seeing my husband pull into that hotel, because he often had business meetings there. However, it was his birthday, and he never did business on his birthday."

While she was telling me her story, I knew how the story was going to end, and my heart was breaking for her. She continued by saying, "When I went into the hotel and glanced around the lobby, I didn't see him. However, my intuition told me to go into the private dining area." She followed her guidance and found her husband dining with another woman and celebrating his birthday. She and her husband separated shortly after the betrayal. The separation lasted for a few months, and then they began couples' therapy. While in therapy, they decided to sell the house and begin again.

As she told her story, she said, "Thank God he didn't sleep with the other woman. Thank God for couples' therapy. And thank God our marriage is slowly being rebuilt."

After she shared her story, I embraced her and held her in my arms for a while. When we talked the following day, I acknowledged her for her strength of heart, dedication to her family, and for showing me the power of forgiveness and the willingness to get to know herself and her husband differently. I also shared my opinion of a man who cheats. She agreed with me and remarked, "That's why I'm so grateful Jason (her husband) didn't have sex with her. I caught them before it happened."

There were a multitude of offers on the property and ours was accepted, not because it was the highest offer but because Rebecca felt a connection with us and wanted us to have our dreams come true. I was happy to get acquainted with Rebecca and learn her story. I was grateful for the miracle and gift of allowing us to purchase their home. Rebecca gave us keys to the property prior to escrow closing. She said, "I want you to have access anytime you want. My only request, please don't sleep there or make any modifications to the property until we close escrow." Of course, we happily agreed.

The first time Peter and I walked into that property, it immediately felt like my home. This was a monumental feeling for me because for the whole of my life, I had never felt a heart connection with a property. Prior to that moment, my experience was I had only lived in houses that were occupied by my stuff and sometimes my family. In what was going to be my home, on the second floor of the property, Peter selected the room he wanted to have as an office. However, to me, when I walked into the room, it felt like a nursery. I had a vision of me holding a baby, sitting in that big bay window and looking into the garden. I thought with absolute certainty, "This will be my first and only HOME! In early September, escrow closed. Peter planned to move in October, I planned to move in April, and in-between we would have our first Thanksgiving dinner in our new home with rented table and chairs, sparsely furnished with our personal items, and we would bring our families together. For the first time, I was really having a home and creating the family of my dreams. Peter would constantly say, "I'm going to give you everything you want. You're never going to want to leave your home or me!" He would also say, "You are my dream come true, just like this house." I appreciated his praise and rarely thought about not being engaged. Actually, it had become a non-issue for me, and I just believed one day it would happen.

The first week in November came, and everyone in the family was excited to have Thanksgiving together in New York. Twelve of my family members were coming from California, and sixteen members from Peter's family were confirmed to attend dinner. It would be a first dinner in a lifetime of Thanksgiving dinners together, or so I thought. I believed I was living my dream and it was only going to get better and better!

I thought about how different it would be living on the East Coast after living my entire life on the West Coast. When the plane landed, I went to the luggage area as usual to meet Peter. Each trip, after closing escrow, I would bring clothes to leave, so when packing, it would be less to move. When I arrived in the luggage area, Peter wasn't there, and that wasn't normal. Usually he would be there with a gift, something to let me know he was thinking of me. I thought, "Perhaps he has gone to the restroom." After about five minutes, I called him. He didn't answer, nor did he call or text within minutes. He usually responded almost immediately to every call and text. After about ten minutes had passed, I saw him briskly walking towards me.

As he approached, I asked, "Are you OK?"

"Yes, I'm good," he said while putting his arms around me and kissing me. "I got stuck at the house with the painter."

"I called you," I said.

"My battery died, and I didn't know it until I wanted to call you and tell you I was going to be late," he said.

We went to the car, and as he opened the door for me, I could sense something was off with him. He was different in a way that was completely unfamiliar to me. Something didn't feel right. However, I didn't say anything to Peter, and I told myself everything was fine. When we arrived at the house, I saw strokes of paint on the dining room wall.

"What color do you prefer?" he asked. "I wanted to have the colors on the wall when you arrived, so you could select one."

I pointed to the one I liked the best and said, "Thank you very much for wanting to make our home more beautiful."

"It's all for you," he replied.

I kind of felt bad about the tone I had used when I questioned Peter about his late arrival to pick me up.

I said, "I apologize for being impatient, and this house is going to be my home as soon as I move in completely."

He accepted my apology and said, "It isn't necessary. I owe you an apology for not being in the luggage area and bringing you something special because you're special to me. And Baby, this house is already your home."

Dinnertime was approaching, and we had developed a habit of going to the same restaurant for dinner each time I was in town. The restaurant had become known between us as "the first meal spot." We both enjoyed this ritual and had become friendly with the owners and a few of the staff.

"Let's go to the first meal spot," I said.

"I don't want to go there tonight," Peter replied.

"Really? Why?" I responded with confusion.

"Don't make a big deal about it. I'm exhausted, and I don't feel like talking to anyone but you," he replied with irritability.

"OK, where would you like to go?" I asked.

"Let's order in," he said.

This was completely unusual. He never liked ordering in. He thought only pizza and Chinese food should be delivered, and he didn't like either. Then he suggested that I go upstairs and relax.

"I think I'll cook dinner for us. How's that?" he said.

His comment was also odd because he liked me in the kitchen with him when he cooked.

"Fine with me," I replied. "I'm not going upstairs," I said with a tone that communicated I was frustrated.

Our communication that evening was pleasant yet distant. We ate and watched television, again, something we never did. Also, Peter was a really good cook. However, the meat was well done, the vegetables were too soft, and the potatoes had too much salt. He never messed up cooking a meal. He was the kind of guy who bragged about every meal he cooked, and he was proud of each meal he prepared.

"Peter, what's on your mind?" I said.

"Nothing. I've told you, I'm exhausted," he replied very snippily.

"OK. I understand you're exhausted, yet there's something you're not telling me," I said boldly.

"I'm making the biggest commitments of my life. Can we just finish our meal, watch the movie, and go to bed? No more probing, OK?" he said with abandonment of conversation.

I knew something was really off, yet I never thought for one second it had anything to do with our relationship.

"Yes, we can do as you asked, and whenever you want to talk, I want to listen," I replied very sweetly.

He concluded, "There's nothing to talk about." I could hear irritability in his voice.

For the next three days, we did things around the house to prepare for our Thanksgiving dinner, and we also went furniture shopping. As much as he tried to act normal, he wasn't. The days we spent together were nice and completely different than any other time we had spent prior, meaning although we were together physically, we were distant emotionally. When I returned to California, we communicated in the usual manner. We still talked on the phone throughout the day and spoke each night until one or both of us were falling asleep on the phone. We were in our rhythm based upon our actions, but still there was an emotional disconnect.

I was back home for about a week when I received a love card from Peter. The card conveyed his deep love, the desire to marry, and his excitement about settling into our new home and the life we would share. The card was beautiful, yet while reading the words, I could still feel the disconnect. After I finished reading the card, I went to place it on my desk and heard the Still Small Voice say, "Peter is with someone else." I pretended as if I didn't hear it, then I heard it again and again. The third time I took control of my thought and said to myself boldly, "That's not true. He doesn't have a minute of time to see or talk to anyone else. He loves me, and I'm just making all of this up because we are going through an emotional disconnect." Although I told myself it wasn't true, somewhere deep down inside of me, I knew it was. Then I tried to convince myself that the reason I wanted to believe it was true (Peter was seeing someone else) stemmed from the betrayal of past relationships. Other thoughts floated through my head, and I couldn't bring myself to discuss them with anyone, particularly because everyone in our circle had a bias towards Peter. However, I did have one acquaintance who I wasn't sure if she didn't like him or if she was envious of our relationship. So, since I needed someone to talk to, I talked to her. Prior to my conversation with her, I told myself not to trust her feedback because I was unclear of her mindset regarding us. After we talked, her conclusion was Peter had never been faithful because all men cheat.

* * * *

Ladies, let's have some for real, real talk; it's imperative that you listen to the Still Small Voice, because it's your life speaking to you, and it wants to give you the insight you may be unable to see. Listening means you're attuning yourself to making Self-Honoring Choices.

* * * *

The truth from the Still Small Voice was confirmed when Kate, the girlfriend of one of Peter's friends, called. The moment I heard her voice, I could tell she had been crying.

"What's wrong?" I asked. There was no response, just sobbing. I asked again, "What's wrong, Kate?"

Finally, after about thirty seconds of crying, she was able to say what she called to tell me.

"This isn't easy for me and all of us feel guilty for not telling you. The reason none of us saw you on your last trip here was because we couldn't face you."

It was as if my heart stopped in that moment. I held my breath and sheepishly said, "What is it?" I was not ready for the bomb she was about to drop.

"Peter is having a relationship with someone else. I don't mean he's having an affair, I mean he's having a relationship, and it's been going on for months. At first, we thought she was just a friend, and recently, we confronted him. That's when he told us they are seeing each other because you need more time to think about moving here and marrying him."

I couldn't comprehend the words, and I definitely didn't want to believe anything she was saying. I quickly got off the phone with her and called Peter. He answered the phone with a tone of joy and excitement.

"Why are you so excited?" I asked abruptly.

"I just finished editing one of our family movies. The release date is Thanksgiving at our home after dinner. I'm so excited that we're having our first dinner in our new home with all of our family. I love you so much!"

His words left me speechless.

"Are you OK?" he asked.

"No, I'm not. Well, yes, I'm OK," I managed to say, although the words were stuck while coming out of my throat.

"You don't sound OK. What's going on?" he asked.

"I'm feeling insecure and overwhelmed," I said while pushing down the thoughts of his possible betrayal.

He responded, "You have nothing to be insecure about or overwhelmed by. I've got you. We are a couple. We are partners."

We continued the conversation for about fifteen minutes. The topic wasn't his betrayal. It was all about the mini-movie he created and how much he was looking forward to our Thanksgiving dinner with our families. I never said one word about Kate's call.

It was exactly eight days before the family would depart for New York. I was flying with them, so we could share the experience of traveling together. I had never traveled with my entire immediate family and cousins. This trip was supposed to be one of the most joyous occasions in my life and filled with a multitude of first experiences. Kate called every day after her initial call. I avoided her calls for days, and then I answered.

"Hello," I said harshly.

"I have something that you may be interested in, and the reason I'm giving it to you is because I know you didn't believe me when I told you about Peter. Here it is. I'm giving you Peter's other girlfriend's number. I think you should call it and ask her. She'll tell you that she's in a relationship with him," she said.

I didn't respond verbally. She said the numbers, and I wrote them down with my hands shaking so badly I could barely discern what I had written. After she concluded giving me the numbers, she asked, "Are you still there?"

My voice was trembling, and I said, "Yes, I'm still here, and now I have to go."

As I hung up the phone, I immediately felt the need to run, so I grabbed the keys and drove to the beach. I parked at my favorite spot that has a perfect view of the ocean and vegetation all around (it's no longer my favorite spot). I sat in the car for about thirty minutes trying to make myself call, while being afraid to call. My thoughts and feelings were swirling in confusion, and my heart was aching.

Finally, I pushed the numbers on the phone. A woman answered the call on the first ring. "Hello," she said.

I introduced myself as my voice trembled. "Hi, my name is RaShawn Renée, and I'm the girlfriend, soon to be fiancée, and one day wife of Peter Gates."

She chuckled and said, "I have no idea who you are or why you're calling me. Who is this?"

I could tell by her tone that she absolutely had no idea about me.

Then she said, "Peter is my boyfriend, and there's no way he would be seeing someone else. I don't know who you are."

It's ironic that she too was committed to Peter and was as completely unaware about me as I was about her until Kate told me. I could barely formulate a thought. I could barely construct a sentence, but I managed to say, "How long have you been dating Peter?"

She replied, "Two months."

It was surprising that she hadn't hung up the phone yet. Perhaps her Inner Knowing kept her on the line. In my desperation to prove to her that Peter was my boyfriend, I said, "I'll send you our correspondence from the past two months between him and me, and you'll know he's my boyfriend, soon to be fiancé, and then husband."

As I was saying those words, she interrupted me and said, "Oh, my receptionist just buzzed. Peter is here. Hold on. We'll let Peter tell me who you are."

I waited on the phone for what felt like an eternity. My tears ranged from streaming down my face to uncontrollable sobbing. I couldn't hold any longer. I hung up the phone and sat in the car trembling and crying. I thought for certain Peter or she would call me back. Neither of them called. After a while, I gained my composure and finally felt able to drive. When I arrived back to my house, I did as I said I was going to do. I opened my email to forward two months of correspondence from Peter. Surprisingly, when I did the search to pull up the emails, they had been deleted. I didn't understand what had happened. However, I later learned that Peter had the password to my email, and he had deleted all our communication.

The relationship I valued, cherished, and trusted was over. I felt devastated, our families were in disbelief, I was no longer in partnership with my prince, and he wasn't charming. Over the next few months, Peter and I tried to salvage, rebuild, and make anew that relationship. Even after the anger and hurt had passed, we tried making it work, but it was never possible. We were completely over.

At one point, I thought my relationship with Peter was the best thing that ever happened to me. Then I thought it was the worst thing that ever happened. Now I know that the relationship was perfect. It wasn't the worst nor was it the best. It is what I needed to grow up and to grow into another level of awareness. If I hadn't experienced the heartbreak and the subsequent aftermath from the relationship with Peter, I might never have learned the value of me. The end of the relationship with Peter left me with a sense of feeling hollowed out, valueless, without identity, and no longer safe, and my dreams were shattered. This would have been the time for me to be alone, reflective, and perhaps seek counsel immediately after that relationship. Instead, metaphorically speaking, I went from the frying pan into the fire by putting myself in a situation that gave me the illusion I was safe and had value. It satisfied my ego to prove to myself and to Peter that I was fine and could do without him. It took years after the relationship with Peter ended for me to understand the subsequent choices I would have to make in the future. It was up to me to identify the next relationship after him, which I thought was supposed to be his punishment, yet I was punished and found liberation.

Today, I hear and respond to the Still Small Voice. I awake next to a man who wholly values, cherishes, and adores me. This man is my husband, and there are no illusions between us. The journey from Peter to my Truth and living powerfully was often seemingly turbulent. I experienced pain, confusion, and lack of personal understanding.

Today, I find value from those seemingly turbulent times and past experiences and I can share my learnings with you. In this way, you may be mindful and know that you are not alone when you find your dream is shattered. I couldn't admit it until I began excavating and examining; I always knew there was Truth and Knowingness at every turn.

✸ ✸ ✸ ✸

I wholly committed myself to him and believed he would marry me.

My actions and my thoughts all reflected my belief.

I commingled and intertwined my entire life with his.

I chose to believe everything he told me even when I felt differently.

I had a feeling Peter was not being a monogamous man early in our relationship, and I made jokes or funny statements like:

"Hey, do you have another girlfriend?"

"If you're dating someone else, just tell me."

I would often make these remarks with a laugh and in jest.

I wouldn't allow myself to hold any thoughts or feelings that weren't in alignment with what he was telling me, even when I felt differently.

* * * *

When a man cherishes you, his actions reflect his feelings consistently.

You are the Prize, and when a man sees the value of you, he will make heaven and earth move for you, because he wants you to experience happiness.

You have to know the real value of *You* before someone else can see it.

Learning more about yourself, understanding your relatedness to men, and making Self-Honoring Choices will create a life of bliss and a sense of fulfillment that is best described as feelings of wholeness, peacefulness, and well-being.

I thought the experiences from Serious Guy Number Three were the best and the worst in my life. Little did I know that Guy Number Four was waiting just around the bend, and I would need to take a darker turn before I rose from the ashes and learned to live powerfully.

CHAPTER EIGHT

ABSENCE AND NEED

The romance was over, the trust was broken, we couldn't reconcile, and we couldn't let each other go. So we decided to schedule one call once a week. I told myself the calls were our way of staying connected and not throwing away a great friendship. For Peter, it was his way of staying connected with the hopes of winning me back. For me, I wanted Peter to feel remorse and know he had lost someone wonderful by cheating, while secretly hoping he would say or do something that would allow me to trust him again. I had a difficult time letting him go.

It was during a scheduled call with Peter that I had my first conversation with Gordon. We met at a business conference where we were both speaking. I was part of the morning discussion, and he was in the afternoon session. After I concluded my presentation, I stayed to listen to some of the other speakers, and Gordon was one of them. I was instantly attracted to his powerful command over the room, the fluidity in which he shared his business knowledge, and the sincerity I felt in his presentation. How he represented himself made me want to get to know him. By the end of the conference, he had my telephone number. He informed me he would call me later in the evening.

Gordon was the first man I was interested in getting to know, since ending the relationship with Peter. When I gave Gordon my number, a feeling of uneasiness came over me, and I thought, "Don't give him your telephone number." I dismissed the thought and continued putting my phone number in his phone. It was about 8:00 p.m. when the phone rang. It was Gordon, and I was pleased to receive his call. I couldn't have known when I answered the phone that I was about to embark upon a multitude of experiences which would include psychological trauma and violence, and eventually would lead me to choose between escape or death. Yes, I paused before I gave him my number. I'm certain it was my *Inner Guidance* saying, "No!" The first call lasted about forty-five minutes, and for most of that time, Gordon was sharing his excitement over us meeting. He said, "I noticed you the moment you walked into the room. I didn't want to stare at you or look too hard because I was certain you had a man; I thought you were taken." From that one remark, I gathered Gordon was a faithful man and wouldn't cheat in a romantic relationship. It was that statement which made me more intrigued to get to know him. I wondered, "Am I ready to date someone? Am I completely over Peter? Should I discuss with Peter my new interest in Gordon? Am I capable of trusting a man in a romantic relationship?" As those thoughts floated through my mind, the phone rang, and it was Peter.

It was our scheduled talk time. I didn't interrupt my conversation with Gordon. I didn't answer the phone. The conversation ended with Gordon and I scheduling our first date. I hung up the phone with the notion, "Gordon is a faithful and committed man." My Inner Guidance had warned me about giving him my number, but I did it anyway. From just one statement, I was defining one of his characteristics, and yet I knew nothing about him. It wasn't more than five minutes after my call with Gordon concluded when Peter called again. Another ten minutes passed, and he called again. This time I answered.

"Hey, I was beginning to get worried about you. Are you OK?" Peter inquired.

"Yes, I was on the phone and couldn't get off. I'm fine," I replied.

"Who were you talking to that you couldn't get off the phone for me?" he asked.

I was silent.

Then he asked, "Are you dating someone else?"

"Dating someone else? What does that mean?" I asked harshly.

He replied, "I'm asking you, are you seeing someone?"

I answered, "I was talking to a man I recently met, and I really like him."

He released a big sigh, paused for maybe five seconds, and then said, "I love you. I know I really fucked up. You have to forgive me and stop playing games. I know you love me, and we both know we want to get back together. If you date someone else, you'll be making the biggest mistake of your life. Please don't do it. Don't date the guy you were just talking to. He's not the man for you."

"You can't tell me what to do," I said in a high tone.

"I'm not telling you what to do. I'm commanding you not to date him. He's not the one for you," he said, sternly.

Each word Peter said moved me closer to the idea that Gordon and I would be dating. As the conversation continued with Peter, I felt something, and I recognized I no longer needed to try to prove my value to him, nor did I need him to do something that would win me back. Perhaps his plea for me not to date Gordon was my victory, and I no longer felt the need to speak to him on a regular basis.

❊ ❊ ❊ ❊

My first date with Gordon was loaded with warning signs that said, "Run far and fast away from this man!" Instead of running, I made excuses for his behavior, discounted the voice of my *Inner Guidance*, and stayed focused on the things we had in common. Then I recalled how impressed I was the first time I heard him speak. I told myself, "Every person can use a little help, and he could be the person I could help. I could make him be a better man."

During our date, he said, "When a man cheats on a woman, it's because he doesn't know he's the man. When a man cheats on a woman, he's the lowest form of scum." His words were the final caveat that captivated my mind, intrigued my heart, and confirmed he would not be unfaithful. It was the first date, and I was already rationalizing, dismissing, and trying to justify behavior that I was uncomfortable with. However, his words kept me in my seat. I was emotionally shattered and didn't know it.

The second date went better than the first, although he drank more than I thought was appropriate. On the third date, he shared stories from his childhood, and with each story, I felt empathy for a little boy who survived such abject poverty, was consistently beaten, was silenced, and had come from a household of mental and physical abuse. I felt amazed he had been able to take himself out of those circumstances and build a successful life, which was fueled by his desire to serve others. Some of his behaviors, language, and habits were my warning signs, yet instead of running in the opposite direction (I really knew he wasn't for me), I moved quickly into a committed relationship with Gordon.

Little by little I surrendered my individuality and attempted to live the vision he crafted for me. Being in a relationship with Gordon meant I had to quell his paranoia that every man was trying to take me from him. I had to constantly prove there was no need for him to be jealous of my male friendships, and I had to calm his insecurities about his relationship with my family. Gordon had a fear of being abandoned and once told me, "Every day I fall in love with you, and I'm afraid that one day someone may see in you what I see in you and try to take you from me. One day you might just want to go, because I didn't take good care of you, or one day you may decide you don't want to be my wife. I'm always going to take good care of you, and I don't want anyone else to take care of you. That's solely my job."

I responded by saying, "Nobody's going to take me from you. I'm not going to abandon you. As long as you're faithful and committed to me, I will be faithful and committed to you."

Gordon wasn't the only one with a fear. I too was afraid. My fear was betrayal and the act of infidelity, so we became constant companions, coupled and committed by fear, not love.

"I'm going to buy you everything you've ever wanted, and I'm going to buy you anything you want, because I want you to have everything. My wife deserves everything." That was Gordon's mantra to me.

One day while strolling down the street of a quaint southern town, I saw an eye-grabbing platinum, diamond, and emerald ring in the store window. I admired the design and the beauty of the ring. We walked into the store, and after about an hour, the ring was mine. Two hours later, the ring was on my finger. The first hour was spent with Gordon negotiating with the store owner. Then it took an additional two hours for them to call a metalsmith to come in to temporarily size the ring for my finger. Gordon wanted to make certain I was able to wear the ring immediately. Later, we would return the ring that was sized for my finger so a ring could be custom-made for me. The ring that I was wearing was temporary, because Gordon demanded that a duplicate ring be made for me because "his wife" wasn't allowed to wear a piece of jewelry that hadn't been especially made for her. I didn't even want the ring. I had only admired it. Yet, it was so important for Gordon to give me everything he thought I wanted. For a while, I stopped pointing out things I liked because I didn't want him to purchase them. Oftentimes the purchases he made on my behalf were financially reckless, and when I would point it out, he would repeat his mantra, "I am going to buy you everything you ever wanted, and I'm going to buy you anything you want because I want you to have everything. My wife deserves everything." I wanted Gordon to be the man of my dreams, and I tried to make him that. I wanted to feel safe and cherished, and be in a loving relationship where I was the priority. However, although he would buy nice things for me and we presented the happy couple faces when we were out in public, everything was quite different inside the relationship. Meaning, when no one was looking, the worst side of him would be exposed and that wasn't part of any dream I ever had; it was actually a nightmare.

It was about one year into our relationship when we traveled to Washington, D.C., for the inauguration of President Obama. One of my longtime friends lived in D.C., very close to the Capitol. She insisted we stay with her and her family. When we arrived at her home, a full meal was being prepared to welcome us and other friends and family members who had come to town for the inauguration. Some of us were staying in her home and others were staying at various hotels and with other people. The day we arrived had been an especially good day for Gordon and me. There were no outbursts of jealousy, no arguments, and I hadn't smiled at anyone whom he felt was inadequate for me to smile at. "I have to teach you how to be with a man because you weren't raised by one"; this was another mantra by Gordon that became a constant about six months into our relationship.

The evening was particularly fun and filled with delicious food, libations, and getting acquainted with the other guests staying at the house. Gordon enjoyed his time that evening. When everyone had left the house and we'd assisted in the cleanup, it was about 2:00 a.m., and we all went to bed. We knew we had to get up very early the next morning because history was going to be made.

As we were about to leave for the inauguration, I received a text from Peter. It read, "Are you here?" I hadn't communicated with Peter since beginning my relationship with Gordon. Although he would text me probably once or twice a month, I never responded. However, on that day after many months of no response, I felt inclined to reply and so I did. My response was, "Yes! I am here with my boyfriend."

"I wish you were here with me," he replied.

Everyone gathered their things and the six of us rode the train together to the Capitol. Within our group was the former husband of our hostess and his son from a previous marriage, who I had met many years prior, along with four other people whom I was not acquainted with prior to that day. Our hostess was going to join us later.

When we arrived at the Capitol, we all went our different ways, which were based upon our access for admission. For so many millions of people, this day was something really special and historic. For me, I was soon to have a life-changing experience and see the president of the United States swear his oath. Gordon and I had been invited to a lavish post-inauguration party by one of his friends who had a lot of political influence. From the time we received the invitation for this lavish party, it had been one of our topics of conversation. Privately, I was slightly nervous about attending the party because there was a significant chance Peter might be there.

After the inauguration, Gordon announced he no longer wanted to attend the party and preferred to attend the party that was being given at the home of our hostess. I was relieved when he made that choice, and although I had been excited about going to the lavish inaugural ball prior, and having the opportunity to see the first lady and the president, I was pleased we were going to the home of our hostess. Like our previous night together, there was lots of scrumptious food, good company, great music, and everyone enjoyed one another. Peter danced through my mind a couple of times, and I was so grateful we didn't go to that lavish party, because of the likelihood was he was there.

During the evening, there was a discussion about a female

artist. My opinion was that this particular artist displayed excellence in her vocal abilities and had a range of musical talents. Gordon had an opposite opinion. The former husband of our hostess and his son agreed with my assessment. Unbeknownst to me at that time, in Gordon's mind, I was disrespecting him. From his perspective, I was on their side and against him. Then another male guest stated his agreement with my opinion. At that point, Gordon got up, walked outside, and started smoking a cigarette. He had supposedly quit smoking months before.

Gordon stayed outside for a long while, and it was probably about twenty or thirty minutes before I went to check on him. As I approached him, I could see the anger on his face. I had seen this look many times before, and quite frankly, on that day, I just didn't feel like dealing with it. I didn't want to tell him again that he had to let go of the pain from his childhood. I didn't want to comfort him by telling him I wasn't going to leave him. I didn't want to sit outside and have another conversation about me not being raised by my biological father. I didn't feel like taking any more of his verbal lashing. I was fed up in that moment with everything I had endured for almost a year.

As I approached him, I asked, "What's wrong?"

He replied, "You're a bitch. I bring you here to have a good time, to give you a new experience, something you've never done before, and you fucking choose to disrespect me. I should leave you here, but I'm not going to because you would like it."

I looked at him eyeball to eyeball and felt defiant. After about ten seconds of the stare down, he said, "Fucking say something!"

I said nothing. I turned around and walked back into the house. I continued the evening with the other guests in the home until I was ready for bed. It was about 2:30 a.m. when I said good night to the five remaining guests still awake and staying at the house.

Just as I was falling asleep, Gordon came into the room saying, "Wake up! Wake up! Bitch! You can stay up all night with those other people, so you better wake up for me!"

I sat up in the bed with the same defiant look I had when I stared at him outside.

"If you were a man, I'd kick your ass right now," he said.

"I'm sleeping right now, and you can fight with whomever you want, but it won't be me," I said with a strong *I'm ready to fight* tone. As I lay back down, I pulled the covers over my head.

He came to my side of the bed and hollered, "Bitch, you better get up right now!"

I didn't move. I didn't say a word. I laid there wide awake under the cover until I heard him snoring. There was a couch at the foot of the bed where he had fallen asleep. I peeked my head from under the cover to confirm that he was definitely asleep, not pretending. I quietly got out of the bed, went into the kitchen to look for something to protect myself with, and found a heavy saucepan. I walked back into the bedroom with the pan in my hand and put it on the nightstand next to me. Gordon had said earlier that if I were a man, he would kick my ass. If he tried to hurt me, I was going to hit him on the head with that saucepan. I fell asleep sitting up in the bed. I awoke lying in the bed with the saucepan in the bed with me and hearing Gordon in the kitchen with our hostess, her daughter, and a couple of other guests staying there. I put on my robe, freshened up, and joined them in the kitchen. Gordon was engaged and acting happy. When I walked into the kitchen, he greeted me as if he was so happy to see me. One of the people remarked, "He loves you so much. You guys are a great couple!" I cringed hearing her words and thought, "I'm living such a lie."

After breakfast, we went back to the bedroom. He closed the door, and as the door was closing, he said, "You're still a bitch, and it's not your fault, because you weren't raised by your biological father. I'm going to forgive you today, but I want you to know I'm getting tired of your bullshit and your disrespect!"

I didn't respond. As he was saying those words, my back was turned to him, and I didn't see it or even sense what he was about to do. When he concluded his statement, he pushed me so hard my body propelled forward and hit the dresser. Before I could think, I reacted in self-defense. I turned around, and with all the strength I could summon through my body, I lunged myself at him, and our bodies collided against the door. I glanced around the room for the saucepan. I wanted to beat him with it, but I didn't see it. Miraculously, it wasn't there, which was a blessing to him and me because I would have used it.

Within seconds, there was a knock on the door, and our hostess was asking from the other side, "Is everything OK in there?"

Gordon replied, "Everything is fine. I dropped the suitcase."

As he was responding to our hostess, he was staring at me with eyes that expressed, "I'm going to hurt you." No words passed between us. I opened the door, walked down the hallway and knocked on Monique's door (the hostess's daughter). I was trembling profusely.

Monique said sweetly, "Come in."

I opened the door and walked into her room. I sat on the loveseat. She came over and sat next to me. She placed her hand in mine and said lovingly and softly, "He's not for you. You don't need to be with that guy."

Then she told me everything she thought about Gordon. She shared with conviction her observations, and she conveyed how I had changed while dating him.

Then she said, "I've never shared with you that I too have been in an abusive relationship. For those of us who have been where you are, we see it. Has he hit you yet?"

Tears rolled down my face, the trembling intensified, and she continued with, "He's an abusive and violent man and will never change. Please believe me, because I'm talking to you from experience."

"What should I do?" I asked.

"I can't tell you what to do. You know what to do, and you have to do it," she replied.

I got up and returned to the room where Gordon and I were staying. He wasn't there. I grabbed my cell phone and returned to Monique's room with the intention of calling Peter. I knew he was in D.C., and I knew he would help me. I thought to myself, "He may have cheated, but he would never talk to me that way or hurt me. He really loved me. He made a mistake, and perhaps this was the time when I would give him a chance to prove his love. Maybe this was going to be the thing that would bring us back together."

I had the phone in my hand, was ready to call, but for some reason, I couldn't do it. I recognized I would be calling the man who cheated and lied to save me from the man who was violent and vulgar.

There was a knock on the door and Gordon said, "What are you doing in there? Come out. I want to talk to you." I have no idea how he knew I was with Monique in her room.

Without opening the door, I said, "What do you want?"

Without warning, he opened the door. He saw the phone in my hand and said, "Are you getting ready to call Peter?"

I thought, "How did he know that?" I just stared at him and said nothing.

He responded, "Well, if you're going to call him, remember, he doesn't want you. He cheated. Nobody wants you except me. Nobody is going to take care of you except me.

Nobody is going to love you like I do. Even your own father doesn't love you." His tone softened, and he continued, "We just have to work out a few things. You know I love you. And now I need you to hurry up and pack, so we can go."

By this time, Monique, who had left the room when he came into the room, was coming back into the room. Gordon said, "We just had a little disagreement. She knows I love her like nobody else will love her, and we're going to prepare to go now."

He extended his hand to help me up off the loveseat. I put my hand in his and stood up. I looked at Monique as she looked away, and I walked out of the room with Gordon. Shortly thereafter, we packed, said our goodbyes, and left.

I sat in the back seat as Gordon drove us. I wept for hours, and as he was driving, he would reach to the back seat to touch my leg, saying, "Everything is OK. Everything is going to be OK. You don't have to worry about anything. I love you so much. I just get outraged sometimes. I don't want anyone to steal you from me."

By the time we arrived back at our house, I was feeling weak, defeated, empty, and violated in a way I had not experienced until that moment. I had never been pushed by a man or anyone else. I had never used my body with the intent of hurting another. I had never thought of needing to prepare to fight. Now as we pulled up to the house, all of these occurrences were part of my life. As Gordon unpacked the car I thought, "I shouldn't have returned to Texas with him. I shouldn't have gone on a second date with him. I should have ended the first date fifteen minutes after it started." I started this relationship wanting to make him my hero, thinking I could change him, seeing the good and dismissing the bad. Any self-confidence, regard, respect, appreciation, or adoration I may have once had for myself at that point was almost all gone. I had given my power away. I had put my life in the hands of someone who wanted to own me, and I had no idea that I was the Prize.

✳ ✳ ✳ ✳

When I speak to women who are having a difficult time letting go of a seemingly disastrous relationship, or they continue having the same relationship, only with a different person, I ask the question, "Do you know that you're the Prize?" Most often, the answer is, "No." Well, let me tell you what I didn't know and so many of us don't realize...

YOU'RE THE PRIZE!

CHAPTER NINE

NEVER ALONE

I knew leaving Gordon was going to have its consequences. Yet I would never have imagined that one of the consequences would be jail.

The sun had yet to rise, and before I opened my eyes, I felt peaceful in a way I hadn't experienced until that moment. It was the greatest sense of peace I had known; it was almost like a dream. It had been about two and a half weeks since the escape from Gordon, and I was staying at Carla's home in the guest room. With my eyes closed, as I was awakening, I heard the Still Small Voice within me say, "You are never alone. I am always with you. Listen to Me above all others." I opened my eyes and repeated out loud my translation of those words, "I am never alone. God is always with me, and I am listening to God above all others."

As those words left my lips, the experience began which

would forever forge me to God by learning what the covering of God REALLY is. The experience took me from believing in God to knowing God with absolute certainty. It started with a thunderous pounding at the front door, and Carla running down the stairs and screaming my name. By the time I got to the bedroom door, I heard the heavy-footed stampede coming up the stairs. I opened the bedroom door, and I was confronted by a swarm of police officers.

"Are you alone? Don't move!" were some of the commands shouted at me! One officer approached me and showed me a picture of myself. He confirmed my name while other officers began searching the room and the remainder of the house. The officer who showed me the picture of myself informed me that the house was surrounded by police, and I couldn't escape.

After the communication from the officer, my first thought was, "Where is Carla?"

I asked the officer, "Where is my friend?"

His response, "You don't need to worry about your friend. You need to worry about yourself!"

A couple of minutes later, I heard, "Clear! Clear! Clear! Clear!" I observed four different policemen saying that word to the only police person without a uniform. I didn't know it at the time, but the man not in uniform was an angel in this experience. The medium-height, brown-haired, ununiformed policeman began walking towards me. It was as if he was walking in slow motion. He never took his eyes off me as he approached. He stopped when we were toe-to-toe, and he motioned for the officer to give him the envelope that contained photos of me.

He showed a second picture from the envelope, and then I knew who had sent the police. Up until that moment, I didn't understand what was happening or why the police were there, but the second picture revealed it all. The picture I was shown was taken by one of Gordon's close friends during a surprise photo session Gordon had set up for us at the beginning of our relationship. When I saw the second photo, I knew the reason for the police being there: it was Gordon's way of punishing me, because I hadn't returned to him. Gordon had tremendous influence in this city and could command whatever he wanted by whomever he wanted most of the time. This moment was another example of his apparent level of influence. As I looked at the second picture, I recalled the words I had heard earlier, "You are never alone. I am always with you. Listen to Me above all others." The words blanketed me, and I knew *God was with me...I could feel it*. With both pictures now in front of me, the ununiformed officer asked, "Are both of these photos you?"

"Yes," I replied.

"Do you know Gordon Collins?" he asked.

I nodded yes.

"Please step away from the doorway and go back into the bedroom."

I did as instructed and walked until I got near the foot of the bed. When I stopped and turned around, the ununiformed officer was standing directly in front of me again.

"My name is Detective Cochran. I am here to arrest you for identity theft and credit fraud."

I have no idea what he said after that. It was as if my auditory function had been temporarily suspended. When his lips stopped moving, I said, "I have to pray and get dressed before you arrest me."

There were approximately five other police officers in the room at the time when I made that statement. They abruptly began shouting things like, "This isn't a fashion show! You aren't in control here! Nobody told you to speak," etc. My eyes were fixed on Detective Cochran when I said, "I have to pray and get dressed before you arrest me." I hadn't taken my eyes off him. We were standing toe-to-toe and staring into each other's eyes without wavering.

Detective Cochran ordered everyone out of the room except two policewomen. There I stood, about to be arrested in a room with two policewomen and Detective Cochran, when he said, "Say your prayers. Get dressed, and I will be right outside the door. When you open the door, we are going downstairs, and I will formally arrest you. Do you understand?"

I nodded my head in acknowledgment and said, "Thank you for letting me pray and get dressed, Detective Cochran."

He nodded his head and exited the room. When he closed the door, I collapsed onto the bed. My legs could no longer hold me up, and the reality of being arrested was momentarily more than I could fathom.

After sitting on the bed for a couple of moments and taking numerous deep breaths, I heard one of the female officers say, "Don't worry. You're OK. He's a good guy, and nothing bad is going to happen to you."

Tears began rolling down my cheeks. I looked in her direction and mouthed the words "Thank you."

"It's time for you to get dressed," she said.

I grabbed the clothes I had set out the night before (not usual for me to take out my clothes the night prior) and I put them on. I combed my hair, put on lip gloss, went to the closet, got a coat, sat down, closed my eyes, and began to pray.

The Lord's Prayer came to mind. It was the prayer I had memorized as a child and had recited many times throughout my life as a demonstration of faith. Since childhood, I had a connection to that prayer, so it was understandable why my mind automatically went to the Lord's Prayer. It was the second prayer I'd ever learned. It was foundational as part of my introduction to faith and conditioning to pray.

As I began to recite the words, "Our Father, who art in heaven..." my mind went blank, and a surge of power went through my entire body. From somewhere deep within me, I heard the name "GOD" and then I heard it again and again..."GOD." It was my mantra, and for several minutes, the name God was repeating itself within me. When I stopped hearing the name of God, I began again reciting the Lord's Prayer. "Our Father, who art in heaven, hallowed be thy name. Thy kingdom come, thy will be done, on earth as it is in heaven. Give us this day our daily bread, and forgive us our trespasses, as we forgive those who trespass against us. And lead us not into temptation but deliver us from evil. Amen."

Something happened while reciting the words of the Lord's Prayer. I felt different than any other time when reciting it. I could feel my heart pounding. It was as if my heart was communicating, "You're alive and God is with you!"

> I opened my eyes, looked at the policewoman who spoke to me prior to my having prayer and said, "You're right. I'm OK, and nothing bad is going to happen to me." As I stood up, she smiled and looked directly into my eyes, saying, "You're right, and I know."

I perceived her as a messenger from God to affirm for me that I was OK. Her kind words, smile, and tenderness, from my viewpoint, were a sign of heaven on earth under the circumstances of our encounter.

I opened the door and Detective Cochran nonverbally directed me to come out of the room and walk ahead of him. At this time, there were about eight police people in the hallways. As I began to walk down the hall to the staircase, the police officers moved aside for me to have a direct path. When I arrived at the top of the stairs and just as I extended my foot to go down, someone yelled, "STOP!" The sound of his voice and the word "STOP!" was jarring because it was the first word spoken to me since leaving the bedroom. I placed my foot back on the landing. I didn't take the next step. While standing atop the staircase, several officers walked around me and lined the stairwell. When the officers were in formation, the officer at the bottom of the stairs said, "Now come down."

As I proceeded down the stairs, I saw three police officers detaining my friend Carla. She was sitting in her office, which was near the front door, and she was wearing her usual beautiful sexy lingerie, while smoking a cigarette with her leg nervously gyrating (she always looked like a glamorous movie star when going to bed). When we finally made eye contact, she said, "You know Gordon did this to keep you from leaving the state. What do you want me to do?"

"Don't call my mother," was the only thing I could think to say. My immediate inclination was to hide what was happening from my mother. I told myself I couldn't bear to put her through more anguish with reference to my relationship with Gordon. Carla didn't respond to my request, and now I was at the bottom of the stairs near the front door.

Detective Cochran, who had been behind me while walking down the stairs, was once again standing in front of me. "It's time to arrest you. Please put your hands behind your back," he said.

"I can't do that. I can't put my hands behind my back to be handcuffed," I said in almost a whisper.

The emotional gravity and shame of being arrested washed over me when Detective Cochran asked me to put my hands behind my back. I felt as if I was going to faint. I reached out for the banister to steady myself, and while in the midst of an experience that could have been the most demoralizing, shattering, and disgraceful event of my life, instead I moved into Holy Communion with God, and knew I was being divinely covered and protected. I didn't succumb or break from the pressure and shame of being arrested.

Then Detective Cochran put his hands directly in front of him at chest level and slowly lowered them down below his abdomen. "What if we put the handcuffs on with your hands in front of you?" he asked.

I was silent and unable to respond as he unsnapped the pocket pouch on his belt and took out the handcuffs. He put one cuff on his left wrist and stepped closer to me. He pivoted his body to shield what he was doing from others and then discreetly showed me how loose the handcuffs would be. He stepped away from me and repeated the question, "What if we put the handcuffs on with your hands in front of you?"

I shook my head yes, acknowledging his terms. I put my hands directly in front of me and then lowered them down to my abdomen area just as he had demonstrated.

Once handcuffed, he put his hand on my arm and we walked towards the front door. About three to four steps away from the front door, another officer said, "Are you ready?" to Detective Cochran. He replied, "Yes." The officer opened the front door, and what I saw was astonishing and unbelievable. There was a sea of police cars; they flooded the block. Carla's driveway had one police car and one blue car in it. The entire drivable street space in front of her home and both neighbors was occupied by police cars. I had never seen so many police cars in one area in my life, outside of a police parking garage.

After a momentary pause, I continued walking until we were out of the house. I stepped off the front porch and stopped. "It's almost over," said Detective Cochran.

"I cannot get into a police car," I said. I watched his eyes move from both the neighbors' driveways to the front of Carla's home and then back to her driveway. His eyes stayed fixed on the car in Carla's driveway for about ten seconds.

And then he said as he pointed, "Can you ride in that car?" I gave him a strong nod indicating yes.

We began walking to the car he pointed at. When we got to the car, I noticed it was the same make and model of the car my mother owned (another confirmation from

God that I was not alone). Detective Cochran opened the door, put my seatbelt around me, and said with a slight smile, "I'll take the scenic route; it takes longer."

Once I was in the car, I observed that many of the police cars started leaving, and for the first time, I noticed that many neighbors were outside of their homes, looking to see what was happening.

As he was backing out of the driveway, he asked, "How did you end up with a guy who would have you arrested?"

I responded without hesitation, "I wanted to feel special and cherished, and I wanted a man who wouldn't have affairs or lie to me."

"That's an honest answer," he replied. He was empathetic and professional, and represented another confirmation that I was being taken care of by God.

While driving me to jail, he talked about his career, his love of the job, and his love for his family, especially his wife. "I'm a lucky man to be married to a woman who puts up with all my shit and still loves me. She's the love of my life!" he said.

I thought to myself, "He's kind to me because he has a great relationship with his wife." I was reminded I wanted to be the love of someone's life, and by settling, I had succumbed to a horrific relationship with Gordon. I didn't know it at the time, but what I really needed was to be the love of *my* life first, before I could be that for someone else.

After talking more about his family, career, and advancing to detective, he informed me that I could sign myself out of jail once the paperwork and arraignment were complete. He also explained the process of what would be happening once I was delivered to jail. He assured me it would only be a matter of hours before I would be released. His communication made my experience of being driven to jail seemingly dignified. He asked more questions about Gordon, and I thought to myself, "I'm never going to see that asshole again, and if I hadn't left him, he would really have killed me." I thought about how from the first date with Gordon that my *Inner Knowing* told me not to proceed with him, and how I continued to dismiss what I was hearing. I had allowed myself to stay with Gordon because I so badly wanted to be in a relationship. It was really ironic and revelatory to have those thoughts as I was being driven to jail. At that moment, I became even more aware of how much I had dismissed my Inner Knowing and myself over my lifetime.

When we were almost at the jail, Detective Cochran's wife called. He pulled over to talk with her. After about five minutes, he stepped out of the car to complete their conversation. I was so grateful his wife had called because it suspended my ride to jail. It also gave me a few minutes alone to take some deep breaths and ask God, "What should I do now?"

When he got back in the car, he asked, "How are you doing?"

"I guess, under the circumstances, I'm doing good," I replied.

"You're doing better than good," he remarked. His tone was softer. I felt like he was somewhat of a friend.

"May I make one call, please?" I asked my almost friend. He looked at me with a half-smile and gave me his phone. I only knew two numbers by memory of people I could call in Texas—one was Carla and the other was Gordon. I thought for a millisecond about calling Gordon because I knew if I told him I would return to him, then whatever he needed to do to get me out of jail would be expedited. I also knew he had influential friends, and he desperately wanted me to return to him. However, I couldn't make that call. I didn't want to hear his voice, and I knew I would never return to him. So, I called Carla. Her voice was trembling as she answered.

"Hello, I'm OK," I said.

She took over the conversation by telling me she had just spoken to Gordon, and he cursed her out for allowing me to stay in her home. She remarked, "He's a horrible man, and I will do everything I can to get you out of there as soon as possible. Please call me as much as you can."

At this time, we pulled up to what looked like a large warehouse. Detective Cochran instructed me to finish the call. As I was saying, "I will call you as much as I can," the call dropped when the large garage-like door opened.

Detective Cochran pulled in, and we were inside a large concrete room with a small doorway. I saw a booth with a very mean-looking woman armed with a massive-sized gun across her chest and a handgun on her hip.

"This is where I leave you. In a couple hours, this will all be behind you. Take care of yourself, and remember, this will be over soon," he said. He escorted me out of the car and told me to stand by the wall closest to the door. "If he'll have you arrested, he's capable of doing anything to hurt you. Don't go back to that guy," he said before getting back in the car.

"Thank you for your kindness," I said with tears streaming down my face.

"You'll be fine," he said.

The opposite wall opened, and he drove away. As I watched him disappear, I had the momentary thought and feeling of, "I'm no longer safe."

The mean-looking policewoman approached me and told me to take off my jacket and shoes, and to take my hair down. I did as she commanded. I placed my jacket across my arm and held the hairpins in my left hand. She watched as I complied.

"Put all that shit down!" she barked. There was nowhere for me to place my jacket and hairpins.

"Where would you like me to put them?" I asked.

"Up your ass or on the ground. What do you think?" she replied.

I folded my jacket and placed it on top of my shoes, and the hairpins on top of the jacket. She instructed me to put my hands up, so she could do a body pat down. When she was done, she told me to pick up my things, put on my shoes, and follow her, which I did. She led me to a space called The Holding Area. In there was an open jail cell to the left and an area set up like a classroom or a lecture hall with lots of chairs and a row of desks to the right of the jail cell.

"Take a seat. You're going to be here for a while," she said harshly and walked away. She probably meant for me to walk into the open jail cell and sit there. However, I went to the chair area and sat in the place that looked like a classroom or small lecture hall. I sat for more than three hours. After a while, I wanted to get up to ask a question. However, I was feeling fragile, and I didn't want to hear someone curse, yell, or speak to me in a manner like the policewoman had done when I entered. I needed to speak with someone who would answer my questions with sensitivity and kindness. When I finally had the courage to get up from my chair, I approached a friendly faced officer.

I introduced myself and asked, "When can I make a call?" I went on to tell her how long I had been there and asked if she knew how long it would be before I could sign myself out of jail.

"I noticed you sitting there, and I didn't know you were a detainee," she said. She directed me to the phones and showed me how to use them. She also said she would look up information about me. I made numerous attempts to make a collect call to Carla. My efforts were in vain as I couldn't get a connection.

The lady near me on my left noticed my difficulty trying to make the call and explained, "If the person you're calling doesn't have a prepaid service to accept collect calls, you won't be able to get through."

to the floor and gave her my seat on the bench. The seating was limited and most of the women were standing up. I introduced myself to her. She barely spoke English, and she was confounded by her arrest. Her name was Grace. I became Grace's caretaker, and Rebecca was mine. Rebecca told me I would be spending the night in jail, and the best scenario would be that I would be released by the evening of the next day. I didn't want to believe her, yet I gathered she must be correct since she seemed to know how things worked there. The officers whom I spoke to earlier had never given me a real timeline. I assessed that the officers I spoke to earlier were trying to keep me calm by not telling me the whole truth. I told Grace everything Rebecca informed me of. Most of the time while in that cell, and our entire time in jail, Grace was inconsolable. From Grace's perspective, she was going to lose her baby while there and be disowned by her family. I became so invested in caring for Grace, I lost track of the passing hours. Finally, the cell door was opened, and we were separated into various groups to be formally charged. Grace, Rebecca, and I were separated, which was difficult for Grace and me. So, as I uncomfortably stood in line with the group I was assigned, I decided to get out of my line and went to Grace's line. Rebecca observed my movement and came to join the line Grace and I were in. We had formed a sisterhood and were committed to caring for one another and staying together. Our bond was not only us caring for one another, it was also a state

I put the phone back on the cradle and thought, "What do I do? I don't know anyone with a prepaid service to accept collect calls. God, please help me!" I said to myself.

After a couple of seconds, I lifted the phone off the cradle and made another attempt to make a collect call. This time the phone connected. "Thank you, God!" I thought. I knew I was having another demonstration that God was with me and I was OK. The connection was muffled, and the call was very brief, yet lasted long enough for me to hear Carla say, "You can sign out on your own recognizance. I'm praying for you. Everything will be all right, and soon you'll be released."

The line disconnected abruptly, and as soon as the call was over, I went directly back to the friendly faced officer. Her name was Officer Tate, and I asked her about signing myself out of jail. She explained the necessary steps for me to be released. I had to be formally charged, go before a judge, and have an arraignment hearing.

"How long will all of that take? I've been here for about four hours, and I haven't seen the judge," I inquired. "It won't be too much longer," she said (which was far from the truth).

After our conversation, I went back to the area where I was previously sitting and sat in the same seat. It was as if I was invisible sitting there because no one said a word to me. Four more hours passed, and I had been there the entire day waiting for someone to tell me it was my turn to see the judge and to sign myself out of jail. While sitting there, I had the experience of continuously reflecting on the blessings of the day instead of the horror. I could have been plotting a life-shattering retaliation against Gordon, and that's what I thought I wanted to do. However, each time I attempted to entertain vengeful thoughts or tried to make him wrong for what was happening, my thoughts would redirect themselves to all the things I had to be grateful for on that day and throughout my life.

There were fleeting moments of anxiety and self-loathing for going against my *Inner Knowing* and staying in a relationship with Gordon. Yet, most of the time, I was counting my blessings.

My eyes were closed. I was silently saying the Lord's Prayer again when Officer Tate put her hand on my right shoulder and said, "You have to go into the cell, now. You can no longer sit here. You were never supposed to sit here. You should have always been in the cell. We let you slide," she said with a smile.

"Does this mean I'm going to be arraigned now?" I asked.

"You have to be formally charged before you can be arraigned," she informed me.

"OK," I said. "The formal charge and arraignm(within minutes of each other, right?"

She didn't reply as she walked away. I suddenl and slowly walked to the cell. There were abou women in the cell. The door was open, and I s entry for a couple of seconds before enterir walked in, there was a woman who was of in(age, and who seemed to be the leader in that j posture and the feeling I had when I saw her g perception that she was definitely in charge after I entered the cell, she smiled at me, loo and down, and said, "I got you!"

The numbness left my body, and I was certa another sign that God was with me. Her Rebecca, and from that moment until I was re kept watch over me. Rebecca seemed to kn every person in that cell, the others that wer(cell during the evening, and some of the offic

By the time the cell door was closed, there had thirty women in there. The cell was probably d about fifteen people at most. The last womar cell before the bars locked was a petite, newl woman. Fear was all over her when she enter She came and stood next to where I was sitting collapsed shortly after entering. I caught her f

of grace. Meaning, while together, we had immunity from the harsh berating and personal indignities we witnessed other women experiencing.

Formally being "charged" meant taking a mug shot, and being fingerprinted, stripped of personal items, and directed to another area of the jail. During this time, I could have really lost my mind, completely forfeited my communion with God, or I could completely surrender to knowing without a doubt...God was with me. I chose the latter.

We were taken to the other area of the jail that felt like absence of life. The thick concrete walls without windows and the attitude of the people working in that area all expressed to me, "Nobody cares about you here. There is no kindness or protection. This is where you go to be forgotten about." Women in that area ranged from being there for months up to over a year. The smell was so offensive to the olfactory nerve that many of us covered our noses and mouths when we entered.

Once in that area, we were lined up and assigned to our cells. I was trembling from head to toe and terrified to go into a cell. Grace didn't want to leave my side. She too was crying and shaking. Then we were all directed to stand in front of our assigned cell. When each woman was in position, all the cell doors opened, and we were instructed to enter. Rebecca could see I was visibly shaken, and I could see Grace was falling apart.

As we were about to enter our cells, Rebecca shouted, "Sleep with your eyes open!" Her words slaughtered the infinitesimal strength I had to take the final steps to enter a cage. My legs gave way as I attempted to make the next steps. The woman already in there grabbed my arm and said, "Don't do that! You don't want to get sick here!"

Her voice and actions were kind. She looked frenzied, and I perceived her as mentally unstable. Rebecca's words played in my mind: "Sleep with your eyes open!" While I was still trying to gather the physicality to stand on my own, a loud buzzer sounded, and all the cell doors closed. When the huge metal doors closed, I was confined and couldn't leave. There was no escape. I had few choices, and this was better than staying with Gordon.

✳ ✳ ✳ ✳

> Gordon thought he was punishing me by putting me there, and I knew I was being liberated by being there. Nothing and no one can diminish you once you decide to make Self-Honoring Choices.

"God, help me, please!" I screamed in my mind. The woman in the cell with me was still holding my arm, although I was standing erect by this time. "I'm not going to be sick. I'm fine, and thank you for not letting me fall to the floor," I said to her.

"You're welcome," she replied. "The first night is the hardest, but after tonight, you won't be scared, and after about six months, you get used to it," she said.

I didn't know what to say so I extended my hand and introduced myself. She looked me up and down, never extending her hand to shake mine. She turned her back to me, bent down, and reached into a pillowcase. I looked around the cell to see what I could pick up to hit her with (living with Gordon had conditioned me to be on alert to protect myself, but I saw nothing to grab to defend myself). She turned back towards me, extended her hand for me to shake, and in her other hand was a Bible. "My name is Hillary, and you may need this. It helps me," she said. We shook hands, and I took the Bible. I was assured again; God was listening to my prayer.

It was the longest night of my life, and I did more than Rebecca recommended. I slept with both eyes open, meaning that I didn't sleep. The night was occupied by Hillary's sane conversation and condemnation of the justice system, sharing stories of her childhood, how she killed her husband, the sexual and physical abuse she endured over her lifetime, and incoherent conversations about what was coming out of the walls. Hillary also shared photos, which included pictures of her daughter and herself taken a year prior. Looking at the pictures of Hillary and her daughter just a year before opened my heart to her, and I felt deep compassion for her. She was vibrant, beautifully dressed, and on a luxurious cruise. Looking at the woman before me, listening to her stories, and seeing the woman she was before jail gave me an understanding of how and why she had become mentally unstable. Her story also made me praise her for her strength, faith, and the endurance she exhibited through her entire life. By all standards, she was a resilient and capable woman who grew up in a devastating environment, was physically abused, and killed her husband in self-defense.

Women who grew up in the manner she did may not have survived childhood. Well, she survived and became the owner of a small business. She married a man who, over the course of their marriage, went from verbally attacking her to physically beating her. She said she never wanted to divorce him because he was the first man to really love her. They separated for a time, went to counseling, got back together, and everything seemed to be better between them. Meaning he stopped hitting and beating her and the verbal attacks were less frequent. Hillary came from an environment where abuse was part of her day-to-day experience. The man she was married to came from a similar background. Hillary's mother taught her that a man has ownership of his woman. From what was seeded in her during her formative years to the life she created prior to killing her husband in self-defense was remarkable. Hillary said, "After we reunited from our separation, I always carried a gun in my purse. It was a habit that began when he started hitting me." The day she killed her husband was the day she was leaving him again, and this time, she was determined never to return. His verbal attacks were at an all-time high, she recounted. She said she knew it was only a matter of time before he would hit her again. That morning she was packing the car and he came home early from work. He was filled with rage when he saw she was leaving! An argument began in their front yard. She tried to get in the car and leave, but he stopped her. She got out of the car with her purse and began briskly walking down the street. She said before she knew it, she was using her purse to protect herself from him stabbing her in the face and abdomen. Her next memory was seeing him lying in the street in a puddle of their blood. She was bleeding profusely from stab wounds, and he was on the ground from her gunshot.

Hillary's story could have easily been my story. I could have stayed with Gordon and experienced his violent behavior and verbal abuses, which could have accelerated to him hitting me (and I knew that was the eventuality if I stayed). Hillary killed her abuser in self-defense. I could've done the same under her circumstances. I'm so grateful I didn't marry him and that my escape was successful. My

Inner Knowing ushered me out of that relationship at the time when I was ready to take action while scared. I'm so grateful I finally had the courage to trust *Me*.

The next morning when the cell doors opened, Rebecca, Grace, and I instantly reunited. Each of us had a lot to say, and from the moment we saw each other, we began telling our stories. Grace began sharing by saying, "I know my husband and his family will disown me and our child as I have caused too much shame." Grace looked like she had been crying all night.

Rebecca told us she had to fight all night with her cellmate, who was trying to have sex with her. And when it was my turn to talk, I said, "We have to be grateful that we will each be leaving here today, and we won't be here for weeks or months."

I recognized during the night that I, and so many women, could be Hillary. I saw what could have been my life. I am certain it was another confirmation from God that I am never alone. I was given a Bible, which I used as my pillow to rest my head during the night while Hillary was talking. Being in the cell with Hillary gave me time to reflect and decide if I was going to live according to someone else's ideologies, or if I was ready to allow God to be my guide.

About two hours after breakfast was served, Grace and I

were called for our arraignments. We were in the first group. Rebecca was called for the second group, and they would go before the judge after lunch. After my arraignment, I was told that my paperwork was being processed for release, and it might take up to two hours. Once I heard that communication, I was beyond ecstatic knowing I was really going to be leaving that place within two hours. After about five or six hours had passed, the two-hour window we were given appeared as if it had been a stall tactic. Grace, Rebecca, and I were returned to the cell area where we had slept. I began getting nervous, and I kept reminding myself that God was with me. When I felt fear and dread at the idea of staying there another night, I would scream the name "God!" in my mind. Hillary wasn't in the cell when I returned. I remembered she said her attorney and daughter were coming to visit her. An announcement was being made about returning to our cells when Hillary entered.

"I'm sorry you have to be here another night, but I'm glad I get to talk to you some more," she said.

I couldn't comprehend why I needed to be there another night. I went to one of the guards to ask why we were still there. She told me to go back to my cell or I would be there for weeks, not just another day. I walked back into the cell and Grace followed me. I broke down, collapsed to the floor, and cried uncontrollably. Grace was now trying to console me. I don't know how long I was crying, but what

I do know is when I stood up, there was an officer with Hillary, and Rebecca stood near her saying, "Please get the items given to you and follow me." We were going home. We, minus Hillary, were escorted to an area where our personal belongings were returned. Then we were taken to another waiting area, where I waited for about six more hours after changing back into the clothes I arrived in.

An officer came into that area, called my name, and told me to follow him. I thought for certain he was escorting me out of jail. I asked if Grace was going to be called because I didn't want to leave her alone.

"You can stay here until she's called if you like, or you can leave after her, which might take another two, three, or four days," he replied.

I chuckled and told Grace, "If your family is in the waiting room, I will talk to them" (she thought they would be there to disown her face to face). We hugged, said bye, and out of the area I went. Rebecca had already been escorted away from us.

I followed the officer to another waiting area that had chairs but that didn't have the cement blocks that were in all the other seating areas. There was a woman sleeping in a chair when we entered. She opened her eyes and asked, "What time is it? When am I going to be released?"

The officer gave her the time, and told her, "You'll be released when it's time."

I said, "Hello," and sat across from her.

She said, "Hi, and you might want to get some sleep. You could be here for a while." She closed her eyes and went back to sleep. It couldn't have been more than thirty minutes before I was being walked down a long stinky concrete corridor. It smelt like a combination of urine and musk. We walked for about three minutes. The more we walked, the more the stench in the air started to dissipate. It was as if the air was getting cleaner as I was getting closer to being released. I took a deep breath in while walking towards my freedom, knowing I was different now, and I could trust Me.

We arrived at the final door. The officer entered a security code. The door began to open slowly. I was free. The first thing I noticed was a big clock directly in front of me. I began calculating the hours; had it been forty-four hours and twenty-one minutes since my ordeal began? Was it forty-four hours and twenty-one minutes prior when I just believed in God? Was it over the course of forty-four hours and twenty-one minutes when I came to know my personal relationship with God?

I was free and felt a sense of peace, truth, and strength that I had yet to experience until that moment.

I stepped through the double doors, went through a metal detector, saw two vending machines, three officers, and Grace's husband; I knew him from her description. I immediately went over to him and confided what Grace had shared with me. He was aware of the absurdity of her arrest and wasn't blaming her or feeling shameful for anything. Grace hadn't disgraced the family, and he wasn't going to divorce her. Grace's husband conveyed he was only concerned about her and felt guilty that she had been arrested. He said, "I am her husband, and I'm always supposed to protect her. I hope she can forgive me." When we concluded speaking, I asked if I could use his phone to call Carla. He agreed, and I stepped outside to make the call. As I walked outside, the fresh air washed over my face. I could actually feel air. While standing there in gratitude for being outside, Carla pulled up, another confirmation that God was with me.

God

The Still Small Voice

Inner Knowing

Inner Guidance

It has always been with me and the same is true for you too.

Do you know this?

PART III

NO MORE HIDING

CHAPTER TEN

ON MY OWN

I left Texas with two hundred dollars in my pocket, void of identity, and returned to California to live with my mother. Leaving Gordon wasn't just a departure from a relationship; it was a physical and mental lifesaving escape. The journey of self-excavation began shortly after my return to California. Prior to my relationship with Gordon, my choices were rooted in survival, wanting acceptance, wanting to fit in, and feeling part of something. While in the relationship with him, I experienced those choices and included the total abandonment of self for relationship. While staying in my mother's home, I made the decision to extrapolate everything in my life, meaning all of my conditioning, so I could fully understand my loss of self. Day by day I made life decisions to be the woman I had never fully allowed myself to be.

One afternoon, while grocery shopping, I realized I was

walking at a frenzied and hurried pace. I felt nervous, the type of nervousness I felt when I lived in Texas with Gordon. A defining experience occurred when I reached the seafood counter.

"Is there anything I can get for you?" asked the clerk.

"No, thank you," I said, which wasn't true. I was there to get salmon.

He smiled. "Let me know if there is anything you need."

As I felt my face smiling back at him, I stopped myself from smiling, nodded my head, and he walked away. In my mind, I had time-traveled back to the local seafood store where I shopped in Texas. It was the place where Gordon would have me followed, or he would follow me. Later, he would condemn me for smiling or showing actions of friendliness, which he perceived as disrespectful. I was more than fifteen hundred miles away, and the memory and feeling of what I once lived was present. I needed to get out of the store immediately. I returned to the car to calm down. Having had the revelatory experience of going from believing in God to knowing God while being arrested and jailed, I did what I knew to do. I talked to God and asked the question, "What's happening here?" The answer came in the form of a question, "When was the last time you were in a grocery store, not concerned about being followed or accused of acting disrespectfully or inappropriately by having an extended conversation or smiling at someone, particularly an employee?"

I began weeping uncontrollably. I remembered the first time I felt hopelessness during one of Gordon's vulgar outbursts when I returned from grocery shopping. I recalled how his jealousy would escalate anytime I was out alone. In his mind, if I smiled at another or spoke to someone he thought was inappropriate, which was any service person, or if I complimented someone he didn't approve of, he perceived it as flirting, disrespectful, and common.

I allowed a solid thirty-minute cry. I reminded myself that I was no longer under the watchful eye of Gordon, and I was free. I went back into the grocery store, and this time, I consciously walked in leisurely. I told myself to be calm, and I went down every aisle in the store just because I could. I was no longer on Gordon's time clock. I approached the seafood counter again and waited for the seafood clerk to finish with another customer. While waiting to be assisted, feelings of nervousness and anxiety began resurfacing. I started having thoughts like, "I'm being followed." Unlike before, I didn't flee. My feet stayed planted in the exact spot.

"Welcome back," said Tom with a smile. I now noticed his nametag. "You looked like you had seen a ghost before. Is everything OK?" he inquired.

I chuckled, "I felt a ghost, and I'm fine. Thank you for asking."

"Great! Then what can I get you?" he replied.

I pointed to the salmon. He packaged it. I thanked him and smiled. The small actions of waiting for Tom to assist me and smiling at him were huge leaps in learning how incremental steps would aid in revealing myself. I was releasing the emotional trauma of my habitual patterns forged with Gordon. By the time Tom handed me the fish, I knew I would no longer allow feelings of nervousness, fear, or anxiety to dictate my responses. I spent an extra forty minutes in the store. I took my time while shopping and talked to anyone I wanted. Metaphorically, I grew a foot taller each time I smiled or had a brief conversation with someone.

"That's one of my favorite recipes," commented the woman behind me in line. "I have cooked it many times," she said, glancing over my shoulder at the recipe I was reading. Our conversation continued, and we ended up walking one another to the parking lot. She was a delightful lady, married for eleven years with two children, and she and her husband were considering a third child. I really enjoyed our conversation and could tell she was really very happily married. She seemingly had what I really wanted, a happy and fulfilling life. She gave me her phone number and invited me to call her anytime.

I wanted to make the dish. Then she asked me to come over, meet her husband, the children, and make the dish together. It was so refreshing to have a simple conversation with someone and not feel as if there would be punitive consequences for the conversation. Life was different.

After our exchange, I asked myself, "What is this feeling?" My immediate response from my Inner Knowing was, "THIS is peace of mind." I sat in my car for a couple of minutes pondering peace of mind. I recalled that I smiled at a man without feeling bad or as if I had done something wrong. I walked down every aisle in the grocery store just because I wanted to. It was then I recognized God was revealing through my experiences at the grocery store what peace of mind was. It had been a long time since, perhaps it was the first time, I was conscious of "its" absence and aware of the feeling peace of mind gives.

Do you feel more dread during the day than joy?

Are most of your experiences based upon survival instead of purpose and/or fulfillment?

Or are you numb and unclear about your life?

I had answered yes at some point to each of those questions.

What are your answers?

One of the gifts of making Self-Honoring Choices is peace of mind and joy.

Driving home, I recognized I was feeling lighter within myself, more joyful, and I knew I was experiencing peace of mind. Later that evening, I cooked dinner, shared time with my mother, and went for an evening walk. While walking, God and I were in communion again. This time a plan for moving forward in my life was unfolding. I was listening to my *Inner Guidance*. It wasn't a long-term plan; it was the first step in claiming my life. There were many situations that needed restoration in my life, and they couldn't all be restored at once. However, they would eventually all be transformed. Long before Gordon was in the picture, I was hiding, being silent, unaware of my power, and living from the paradigm that was an out-picturing of my conditioning.

> No matter where you are in your life at this moment, you can begin excavating, examining, and releasing the conditioning that doesn't support you, and you can become who you truly are!

Few people knew I was in California, and it was time to begin making my presence known. I made a list of people to contact and began making amends wherever necessary. It took a year to complete, and through the process, little by little, I learned to trust myself more and attune my listening and guidance from God. Within a year, I had gone from running out of a grocery store because I felt the presence of a ghost when a man smiled at me to becoming a woman who was enrolled at a local University, studying Spiritual Psychology, and making choices in alignment with my personal truth. I was preparing to delve more into the discovery of me, and I no longer cared about fitting in, belonging, or being accepted by abandoning myself to get love. I was ready to reveal myself as the woman God created me to be.

> If you are living in your familiar or societal conditioning and not experiencing the exuberance of life, there is so much more for you to have. You too can become the woman God created you to be.

The program at the University was a two-year curriculum. The first year opened and exposed me to my life in a way I had not known before. It also gave me the courage and strength to be fully seen. While in that first year of the program, I pursued and was offered a tremendous opportunity for academic advancement. It was something I had wanted to accomplish for a long time. Then I asked myself the hard question after acceptance: "Was I going to fulfill my ego and accept the offer, or was I going to stay and complete the work at the University?" A defining moment came when I stood in front of my classmates, more than 250 students, told the story of my life prior to the education I was receiving there, and explained my quandary regarding the choice I needed to make. "No matter how great this opportunity from the other university is, my ego really wants it; and it would advance my intellect. However, I am at the point in my life where I must learn how to live, and from my perspective, it is by being part of this community. I have never experienced learning at a level which is uniquely crafted for the intellect and personal development of each individual to understand life, living, uniqueness, and commonalities by learning of themselves. So instead of nullifying my learning and moving to another academic program to expand my intellect from an egoic desire, I am choosing to stay here, learn me, how to live and intellectually expand, because my heart and soul deem it necessary. There is nothing more important than the discovery of how to live a fulfilling life."

As I concluded, I received a thunderous applause from my classmates. I added, "I am on the course of self-discovery and committed to creating myself as a woman whom I can admire." Making that declaration and saying those words in front of my classmates was an awe-inspiring experience and another step towards me learning how to express myself fully. I am certain each of us has the capacity, and when the desire is there, we can stand in the power of choosing fulfillment of Self.

The coursework was rigorous. The experiential learning was heart-opening, emotionally and psychologically challenging, and it provided me the education and tools to create a more fulfilling life. I am so grateful that at a

Choice Point, I chose me. The decision was made from my heart. Choosing me garnered a standing ovation from my classmates because I was choosing Truth. Life is really good and more beautiful when you get to see who you really are.

> When was the last time you chose to learn about you?
>
> Do you fully trust yourself and love yourself?

After graduating from the two-year master's program in Spiritual Psychology, it was time to reenter the workforce. I hadn't had a job, meaning employee/employer relationship, since my twenties. All of my working experience had been as an entrepreneur, primarily in the real estate industry. My natural inclination was to take real estate courses, pass the exams, become an agent, and then become a broker. I knew I could earn a good income and make a great career. So that was my mindset: to do what was familiar to me. However, my plan wasn't God's plan.

One night, prior to going to sleep, I heard my Inner Guidance, which communicates as the Still Small Voice within, say, "Get a job." I heard it clearly. I asked, "Did you say, get a job?" "Yes!" was the reply. The next day, I went to a talk being held at the University. A gentleman approached me.

"We've been talking about you all evening because my

partner needs to fill a position at his company, and he has identified you as the perfect person for the job."

"Are you sure I'm the person you were talking about?" I asked.

"Yes! You're RaShawn Renée. You are the woman who stood in front of your class declaring you were living differently and choosing to know yourself above anything else," he replied.

I was in awe and reminded of how my Inner Knowing knew best, and God was guiding my life. The job was in property management, and it was exactly in my area of experience and expertise. It was more than just a job; it came with a good income, a biweekly salary, great incentives based upon performance, medical insurance, and corporate matching funds. In addition, my office was located in a high-end residential community, and I had the opportunity to interact with clients from all over the world. My Inner Guidance and making Self-Honoring Choices had positioned me for the absolute perfect job. I had to take a series of personality and competency tests, provide a résumé, agree to a comprehensive background check, and be interviewed by a third-party company who was hired to vet all candidates prior to employment being executed. Every step of the process was extremely scary for me! I didn't have a résumé. I was afraid to take the series of tests, and I was mentally tormented by the idea of a background check, knowing it might reveal the aftermath of leaving Gordon by showing I had been arrested. I was fearful at every juncture of the hiring process, yet no matter how fearful I was, I kept moving forward with what was required to be a candidate for employment. After weeks of moving forward while being scared, I was hired. Wow!

The day after being hired, I pretended it was my first day at work and drove to what was going to be my new office. I wanted to have a mock day to estimate timing for dressing, traveling, and any other occurrences that might be part of my morning routine when I began my new job. Once at the building, I acquainted myself with the surrounding properties and the community. I wrote notes so I could do an analysis of the comparable buildings. I enjoyed every moment of my self-imposed preparation. I looked forward to beginning a new job that had the possibility of being a career. I had never thought of or seen myself as an employee. Now, with new thinking and making different choices, I was seeing life through a different lens.

The first day of work resulted in lots of training, paperwork, and meeting my colleagues. Day two was shadowing various employees, and day three was my solo day, where I did all the work independently and was critiqued at the end of the day by my superior. It didn't take long before

I had command of my role and responsibilities, and was outperforming those in lateral positions. Within the first couple of months there, I began receiving handwritten notes from residents and potential residents who had previewed as consideration for residency. The messages in those notes communicated their observation and appreciation of my knowledge, professionalism, and personable attention to them. I treated our leases and prospects as if they were living in my home. I listened to their needs and desires, and if our property wasn't a fit, I would aid them in finding a property to accommodate their individuality. I enjoyed the notes and constant positive feedback I received from my efforts. However, I rarely shared the accolades with my coworkers or anyone else. While having a job and making Self-Honoring Choices, I grew secure within myself and was no longer starved from the yearning to fit in, feel special, or seeking the constant approval of everyone around me.

My direct boss, the man who had identified me as a perfect fit for the job, called me into his office to compliment my work performance and the care I was giving the residents. He talked to me about the possibility of managing my own building and said, "All of corporate is looking at you. You're the best, next to me, we've ever had."

I was thrilled and absolutely delighted about this conversation! While in his office, he received a call from his boss, and they realized my background check wasn't in the file. He was advised that I needed to sign another release form, and they would begin the process of obtaining another comprehensive background check. When I heard this, fear clenched every part of me! I was scared and so frightened!

While in fear I said, "Sure. Of course, I'll sign the form again."

After work, no matter how hard I tried, I couldn't release the feeling of fear. Prayer didn't help. Silent prayer didn't help. Praying out loud didn't work. Trying to change my thoughts was of no assistance. I couldn't shake the thought that my background check was going to cause me to be fired. Feelings of unworthiness and shame took me on a loathsome downward spiral.

The next morning, I felt better than I had the evening before, yet something still was amiss. I was ahead of my normal schedule for preparation to work. So I decided to open my mail, *something I hesitate doing just because I don't like opening mail*. I hadn't looked at my mail in about two weeks. When I opened the second envelope, there it was, a letter from the third-party company informing me that due to a legal situation in Texas, I wouldn't be a fit for the corporation. The letter also informed me that they were making the recommendation to my employer that I be immediately terminated. After reading this devastating news, I sat on the bed and cried. I had the thought, "Gordon has ruined my life." As soon as I had that thought, I heard two things: "Call your boss and go to work." I didn't do either immediately, and instead I called a cherished friend whose opinion I have respect and regard for. I told her what had just happened.

She said, "You should go to work. Don't say anything, and if you're going to get fired, you're going to get fired. Let them do it. Don't give them any additional information. You don't want to sabotage yourself. They might never find out, and you're doing a great job there. They need you."

I hung up the phone agreeing mentally with her recommendation, yet in my heart, I knew I couldn't do as she recommended. I had learned from past experiences like writing that check, having a second date with Gordon, and so many other experiences that when I do opposite of my heart, my Inner Guidance lets me know there is going to be suffering at a deep level. I picked up the phone and called my boss. I read him the letter, and at the conclusion of reading it, I said, "What shall I do?"

"Don't come to work! I can't have you working here!" he said very forcefully. His tone was harsh and direct.

I had never heard him speak to me or anyone else with that tone. I wanted to crawl into a hole and let this experience pass. However, somewhere between making the call for advice and calling my boss, I knew I was going to do as I had been guided. So, although scared, I picked up my work tote, got in the car, and drove to work. When I pulled into the valet, I was so nervous getting out of the car that I was trembling and could barely exit the car. I greeted everyone somberly, which was not my usual disposition. I went directly into my boss's office and closed the door.

"What are you doing here?" he said with disdain.

"I came to do my job, and if corporate wants to fire me, let them fire me. I'm great at my job. You even acknowledged that. If they are shortsighted, don't see my value, and are willing to let me go without hearing my story, then I don't want to work for this company anyway!" I said with great conviction.

Even I didn't know I was capable of speaking like that and speaking so powerfully for myself. I was horrified, yet I stood up for myself. My knees were trembling. I was profusely sweating, and with all of that, I chose me. I responded while in fear and made another Self-Honoring Choice. I was no longer being silent. This was another time where I clearly recognized I was becoming the woman God created me to be. I was releasing the conditioning that no longer served me.

"OK. Go to work, and we will wait to hear from corporate," were his final words.

We were especially busy that day. I hardly had time to feel dread, shame, or pleased with myself for speaking up. When the day concluded, my boss called me into his office.

"Thank you for coming in today. I don't know what we would do without you, and whatever happens with corporate, I will support you here or help you get another job. You are an excellent employee!" he exclaimed.

I was thankful and grateful! "Can I hug you?" I asked.

"Yes," he said.

While hugging him, I said, "Thank you for believing in me."

"I don't believe in you. I know you and I see who you are," he replied.

By listening to my Inner Guidance, I had a great job, learned not to be silent, made amends in relationships, was paying off debt, and learning Me. Life was changing, and I felt wonderful! Corporate never called that day or any other day. I worked there until I was ready to leave. I didn't make the choice to resign until I was guided by my Inner Knowing to say yes to one of my most heartfelt dreams.

I was led out of conditioning, survival mentality, and egoist responses by the grace of God, by deciding to make Self-Honoring Choices. I learned by trusting, obeying, and taking action given by my Inner Knowing (God), Inner Guidance, the Still Small Voice...You know what I'm referring to. You've heard it. It's the guidance that informs you to do something out of your comfort zone or says, "Don't do that." It's the voice that's always with you. Many times in the past before I learned to make Self-Honoring Choices, and all the other things we've discussed, I would listen when in crisis, and only sometimes take action. When the crisis was remedied, I would return to the dismissal of myself and continue to make choices of a similar kind that had put me in the dilemma. Thinking that represses, marginalizes, or is unexamined isn't the thinking that will free you. I learned to think differently. Instead of responding from unexamined conditioning, I learned about the fullness of me by excavating my conditioning.

When I resigned from my job, I was ready to begin a new chapter in my life, and this chapter would include peace of mind, Self-Honoring Choices, being the Prize, understanding my value and power, and sharing myself fully.

Do you know you are the Prize?

Are you making Self-Honoring Choices?

Are you being a Mother-to-Another?

Do you understand your Power?

If yes, congratulations for knowing the Truth of who You are!

If no, are you willing to begin now?

This is your time to begin knowing who You truly are, or it's your time to continue living in the magnificence of You.

I LOVE YOU!

CHAPTER ELEVEN

CHOICE POINTS

I've listened and talked to hundreds of women from various backgrounds, and I've found a common thread, which connects us and divides us: it is the erosion of making Self-Honoring Choices. This is our commonality and it's perpetuated by the conditioning to hide the essential truth of ourselves. Through our societal and familial conditioning, we are taught to be quiet and marginalize ourselves. Sometimes it's called "being ladylike," and at other times, it's called "being private," or "protecting the family." We're communicated to in a myriad of ways to hide. Hiding aspects of yourself may be the only way you've been trained to live. However, what I know for certain and want to share with you is once you begin to reveal yourself, it becomes abundantly clear that your new Way-of-Being is a pathway to a fulfilling life. Being on the path of self-discovery and awareness not only produces a harmonious life, it allows you to become intimate with yourself. It is the most scrumptious, delicious, amazing, fulfilling gift.

On the journey, you will learn to accept all of You, and you will wholly love yourself in spite of whatever you've gone through. By releasing unconscious conditioning and seeing yourself with new eyes, the view from which you see You will facilitate Power and then You will begin to liberate yourself from stagnant thinking. It's at this point when character development begins to reshape itself, and the Truth of who You are and the person you've always dreamed of being are revealed. If you've never dreamed of who you wanted to be, a vision of who you can be will begin to develop. It's another by-product of becoming conscious and releasing the conditioning that no longer serves you. The splendidness of learning to cherish and value yourself independent of material circumstance and to see yourself as you can be is a journey of Self-Love.

Choice Points are the bridge from your old paradigm to the new conscious and fulfilled Way-of-Being and living.

Choice Points are those necessary situations that allow us to see if we are changing or not.

They become the compass that indicates if we are still living with unconscious thinking and unexamined conditioning, or if we're creating a world of delight by making choices of honor and releasing the patterns that don't contribute to a fulfilling life.

Desire can sometimes make a Choice Point difficult to see. One of those tests came while I was on a date, post-Gordon. It was the second date, and I liked the company of this man very much. At the end of the date, he kissed me on the cheek, and I returned the kiss. Then he attempted to kiss me on my lips, and I pulled my head back to make certain there was no lip contact.

"What are you doing?" he remarked.

"I'm not ready for the intimacy of a connection regarding my lips," I responded.

I almost couldn't believe those words came from my mouth. Then I heard my Inner Voice say, "Good job." I smiled from what I heard because I wasn't being silent. I spoke up for myself. I made a choice, which honored me, and it was a Choice Point, since that was his expectation. The irony of the choice was after choosing, I didn't want him to think I was a prude, nor did I want him to think I didn't want to go out with him again. The thoughts that entered my mind when I made the choice not to kiss him had no validity or power to change my choice or make me silent. This Choice Point indicated I was no longer the girl who desperately wanted to be accepted and was willing to go along for the benefit of others. I was making a Self-Honoring Choice and developing the constitution that was becoming the blueprint and scorekeeper of the new life I was creating, choice by choice.

He called me two days after our date and asked me out again. While on the phone, he said, "I wasn't sure if I was going to ask you out again, because I thought you were playing hard to get, and I don't like playing games."

He also communicated he had talked to his father and was informed by his dad, "She's a woman who respects herself. You need to call her right away, and hopefully she'll go out with you again."

I was pleased to hear the feedback he received from his father and even more pleased Dale said, "My dad is correct. You're a woman who's worth the wait." His words affirmed I was being seen, heard, and validated by a man I had gone on dates with.

I accepted Dale's invitation to go out on another date. While on that date, Dale said, "I've never taken this much time to get to know a woman without having any physical contact other than a kiss on the cheek." I smiled, and he continued, "You're really different, and I'm willing to take my time to get to know you."

"Thank you for allowing me to be the first, and hopefully I won't be the last. This should be your standard, and I'm enjoying getting to know you too," I responded.

"I'm going to take you to one of my favorite restaurants on our next date. My family has been going there since I was a kid. Would you like that?" he asked.

"Yes. That would be nice," I answered.

Three days later, we were on our next date. While walking into the restaurant, another patron opened the door for us and complimented me on my dress. We went to the hostess station to check in, and the man who had opened the door approached us and said, "Hello." In unison, we replied, "Hello," and the maître d' escorted us to our table. Shortly after being seated, Dale received a call regarding a patient and excused himself from the table. The moment he left, the man who had opened the door for us came to where I was sitting. He wanted to know my name and asked if Dale and I were married. I politely told him I was on a date, thanked him again for opening the door, and invited him to leave the table (something didn't feel right). The guy wouldn't go and was trying to convince me to take his number, since I wouldn't give him mine. After several minutes, I was at my threshold of tolerance. I got up from the table to retrieve the manager with the intention of having the manager rid him from the restaurant.

As I got up, Dale was walking back, and the guy walked away. I informed Dale of what happened and told him I was headed to get the manager as he was returning to our table. The manager came to our table as I was telling Dale the story. Another guest observed I was being disturbed and had reported it. The manager apologized profusely and told us he would pick up our tab for dinner.

Throughout dinner, Dale wasn't his usual self. I asked him at least twice, "What's wrong? Are you OK?" He replied, "Nothing, and I'm OK."

He seemed irritated by my presence and unable to enjoy the evening. When Dale was driving me home, he finally communicated his thoughts, which included his perception of my disrespect for him by not coming to get him the moment the man approached the table. He indicated I showed a lack of regard that was compounded by me getting up to get the manager and not coming to get him first. He also thought I gave the man an unnecessary smile when he complimented me on my dress, my red nail polish was too provocative, and I shouldn't have said we weren't married, unless I wanted to give the stranger my number. By the time Dale pulled up in front of the house, I could barely wait for the car to stop. He concluded by saying, "I hope you understand my position. I am a man who needs my woman to respect me and who I am. Do you know how many women want to date me, would like to be seen with me, or dream of me talking to them?"

Without acknowledging his questions or comments, I got out of the car as quickly as I could. His behavior was recognizable from past experiences, and he was acting too similar to Gordon. Another Choice Point was present. Would I continue dating him or not? Those were the choices. The following morning, I received a text message and two voice messages from Dale, apologizing for what he said. He blamed his words on fatigue, and being acutely on guard regarding a woman's behavior. He told me he had much to offer, and he never wanted to be made a fool of. I didn't respond to his text or voice messages. Over the course of the next week, he sent flowers, wrote a poem, and sent a thoughtful letter, which was delivered with champagne and a note that read, *"Please forgive my ignorance. My dad is right, and I want to continue seeing you. Let's make up with a toast and whatever else you like."* When reading his note and reflecting on his numerous attempts to communicate an apology, I could sense myself rationalizing his actions. My ego was flattered by his attempts to convince me to go out with him again. I told myself, "I should forgive Dale and give him another chance." I thought I was resolved with the fact I would never see him again based upon his comments in the car on the drive home and his attitude at the restaurant. However, my "should voice" became unceasing when telling me to give him another chance. The truth was apparent, yet difficult. Deep within, I knew I shouldn't see him again, and I knew I was no longer willing to accept behavior that was contrary to me feeling good or being treated as I am the Prize. I had learned from an accumulation of experiences that when a man speaks to me, or any woman, in the manner that Dale had spoken to me, he had no place in my life. It should have been an easy choice based upon what he said, yet it was a seemingly difficult choice. I, like many women, are taught to forgive, and I was breaking the conditioning of men treating me haphazardly. I had to choose him or me, and I chose me...Yay!

My compass informed me that this was a defining Choice Point. It had become abundantly clear that I had changed and was living as a woman of value who makes Self-Honoring Choices. The "should voice" was the test to confirm or deny if I was choosing differently, and I was; this is what Choice Points do. I confirmed I was different by the choice I made. I wrote him a lovely note, meaning there was no upset or making him wrong in the communication. I sent him flowers and ended our entanglement. Writing the letter and sending it was more for me than for him. I was proving to myself that I was learning to treat myself well and make choices that honored me. I didn't allow the thoughts that were seeded in my formative years and reinforced by society to have any bearing over me any longer. I had moved away from the mindset which kept me in the cycle of being unfulfilled, hidden, silent, feeling not enough, and fearful. Making one choice at a time and staying committed was, and continues to be, vital for creating a Life-of-Delight. Choice Points, after excavation, took me from experiences of existing and surviving to thriving and being fulfilled.

It is through self-knowledge when Choice Points can reveal the Truth of who we are. Remember, none of us are broken, so we don't need to be fixed or healed. We simply need to release the mental shackles of unexamined conditioning and be willing to accept the real Truth of who we are. We must be willing to accept that which we desire from our true self and release that which doesn't add joy or contribute to creating a fulfilling life.

A couple months after dating Dale, I went out with a man who I thought was especially nice. On our sixth date, he shared a deeply personal family story. All I could hear inside of me was, "This guy is for me." I appreciated the way he was raised, the loving relationship between him and his parents, the camaraderie of him and his siblings, and the loving communication that seemed to exist within the dynamic of his family. He was perfect (perhaps). He shared how his life got derailed when he got hooked on drugs. His addiction broke his mother's heart, his whole family was in disbelief, and everyone rallied to support him through his drug abuse. The story he portrayed of his family, friends, and the way he was living was inspirational and deeply heartfelt. At the point when I came into his life, he had been drug-free for five years. I knew I could help him and make his life even better. He would often say things to me like, "I didn't know angels like you could appear magically. How is someone as sweet as you are? You are the missing piece to my puzzle." In each conversation with him, I always felt special, like he was sharing his heart and perhaps I was the missing piece of his puzzle.

One day he picked me up in a different automobile. It was the shell of a Range Rover, and the interior of the car looked like several cars combined. It was like one of those movies I had seen when cars would come back from what is called a "chop shop" and all pieces of the car are different.

"Whose car is this?" I asked.

"This is my real car," he said as he looked down with embarrassment.

"Where is the fake car?" I asked. Meaning where was the Mercedes he was picking me up in on each date up until that time.

"I returned it," he responded.

"Whom does the other car belong to?" I inquired.

"It's a family car," he said.

I could see sadness and shame move across his face. I felt kind of bad for giving so much attention to the Range Rover-ish car.

"I didn't want to disappoint you, and I didn't know how to tell you. So today I brought my car, so I could tell if you really like me. I wanted to make certain our friendship is real and not just superficial," he expressed.

"I'm confused. Don't present something as yours if it's not." I remarked. "Today you get a pass for not being truthful with me. However, remember, you only get one pass, because if you lie to me or purposely omit telling me something, I'll be finished with you."

He smiled. The sadness and shame were removed from his face. We hugged, and I got in the car. We went out dancing, and before the night ended, we agreed to see each other later in the week. The evening had begun very uncomfortably and concluded with him sharing more about his past and saying, "I'm so happy we met, and now I feel like I can tell you anything. Thank you for not judging me."

When he dropped me off at home, he apologized for not telling me about the car and assured me he would never conceal anything again. He asked if it would be OK on our next date if he could cook me dinner. He said, "Do you know I'm a really good cook? May I cook for you on the next date?"

"Yes. I would like that," I replied.

We said our goodbyes, and I went into the house. Before going to bed, I recounted a couple of stories he told me while on our date. He talked about his hectic and fast-paced business, the culture within his industry, and the recreational practices of his colleagues, which led him to drugs. At dinner, he told me he had sold almost everything in his house when he was on drugs, and five years later, he had yet to totally refurnish the house. Thinking about what he said or shared had made me prepare myself that his home might have little or no furniture.

✴ ✴ ✴ ✴

It was Friday night, the night he was cooking dinner for me. I called him to let him know I was on my way and to confirm that he still didn't want me to bring anything, although I was bringing a surprise dessert no matter what he said. I didn't think it appropriate to arrive empty-handed. After being on the road for about thirty minutes, I was turning onto his street, and there it was, a magnificent craftsman home. From the car, while on the opposite side of the street, the house looked well maintained. However, as I approached the walkway, I noticed storm-like shutters covering the windows, which isn't typical for that style of home or a home in Southern California. He opened the door with a huge smile on his face and greeted me with, "I'm so happy you're here!"

It was obvious he had been watching me approach the house. When I crossed the threshold and entered his home, there was a funny smell in the air. I guess my face conveyed I could smell the aroma.

He said, "I'm cooking gumbo, since your family has southern roots, and I scored a great recipe from my neighbor."

I smiled, saying nothing, knowing the smell wasn't the smell of any gumbo I had ever smelled in my lifetime. We then walked into the living room. I was aghast! The couch appeared to be so dirty I wouldn't sit down.

He asked, "What's wrong?"

I didn't want to say what I was thinking: "The sofa looks so disgusting I might get a disease by sitting on it." Instead, I asked, "Is there somewhere else we could sit?"

We walked into the kitchen, and what I saw there couldn't be explained. Most of the cabinets had no doors, and the kitchen table had a tremendous crack. I said, "What's going on here? Why does your home look like this?"

His reply, "Since we met, I decided it's time to get serious about redoing my home. Up until I met you, I had just been focusing on rebuilding my business and taking care of myself."

As he was talking, he opened a bag and showed me the new Tupperware he purchased so that I would be able to take gumbo home for myself and give one container to my mother and another to my cousin. I had conveyed earlier that my cousin would be sleeping over, so I thought it especially kind for him to have containers of food to give them when I returned home. This man had a wonderful heart and was rebuilding his life, but he wasn't for me. I knew if I didn't stop dating him right then, I would allow myself to get hooked in and put my focus and energy on helping him rebuild his life. I had to stop myself from taking responsibility and wanting to fix him.

I said in the kindest way I knew how, "I'm very uncomfortable here, and as much as I like you, appreciate your thoughtfulness, and would really like to date you, I have to go."

He gave me a look. It was the same look he had given me while standing outside of the Range Rover-ish vehicle.

He felt shameful, and I felt bad for having to make that choice. I began walking to the front door, and he followed.

I opened the door, walked out with him standing at the doorway, and said, "I'll talk to you later."

He didn't respond. He stood in the doorway with his head down.

On the drive home, I called a dear friend, Harry. Harry was a witness and had a front seat to the excavation which was occurring in my life and had taken me from a woman in a violent relationship to the woman who was living and learning whole-self acceptance. I shared with Harry my experiences at Dale's home. I also told him about a few of our previous dates.

He said, "Do you see any patterns here? Haven't you done this before? Haven't you aided a boyfriend to build a business? A life? And committed yourself to another and lost your identity?"

"Yes, kind of," was my reply. "But Dale is different."

"Wow! Well, if Dale is different, then you're the same," Harry replied. His words pierced my heart and my mind, and gave me clarity. They were exactly what I needed to hear. It was abundantly clear this was another Choice Point.

The next day I called Dale and told him, "As much as I would like to continue going out with you, it's not possible."

"You're pretentious," he responded by interruption.

I replied, "OK, whatever you say. I'm not going to defend what you just said," I hung up the phone.

Later that afternoon, Dale called and asked, "May I come over and talk to you?"

I thought about it for about two seconds and replied, "Thank you for wanting to come and talk to me, but it isn't necessary." I never spoke to Dale again.

When we make Self-Honoring Choices, we grow incrementally more dynamic, meaning our personal power and the manner in which we treat ourselves, and allow others to treat us, moves us to a higher standard. Once you recognize who you are and who you have been, the evolution of you seemingly is quickened. Your life begins to manifest dreams and fulfill desires. In addition, one day, you'll hear yourself say or do something and recognize it's a huge leap from where you once lived inside of yourself. You recognize how your thinking is different. Remember, all progress is incremental. There will be times when you have to remind yourself that you make different choices. You may have to call a friend who will support you in remembering that you make Self-Honoring Choices, or it may become seemingly automatic. Regardless of which way it comes, you will know by the out-picturing of your life when you're changing.

My Choice Points quickened with each Self-Honoring Choice. This became even more evident when on a date with a very well-known cardiovascular surgeon whom I had been acquainted with for many years. In the past, he had asked me out numerous times, and I would always say, "No," for reasons unclear to me. I thought he was the perfect picture of a husband and father. He seemed like a very nice person, he played the piano, was an artist, dressed impeccably, was extremely successful in his career, and was philanthropic. I thought he was "the package." After running into him at a friend's dinner party, we exchanged numbers. I hadn't seen him in years. He called, asked me out on a date, and I said, "Yes."

My no had changed to a yes. I was learning my value and becoming more aware; I am the Prize. On our first date, while sitting in a very fancy restaurant and listening about his pathway to success, he shared his desire to be married, have a family, and how this first date could be the beginning of a lifetime partnership. The conversation was flowing beautifully, and I could see myself in the vision he was communicating. Then, out of nowhere, he told me how big his penis was. With conscious thought, I immediately took my napkin from my lap, folded it, placed it next to my wine glass, and stood up.

"Where are you going?" he said.

"This date is over, and you need never call me again."

I walked to the front of the restaurant and asked the maître d' to call a taxi for me. This restaurant was so fancy that they had a car service on call. Within minutes, a nicely attired driver was coming through the door for me, and Dr. Big Penis was still sitting at the table. He had called my cell and sent me a text demanding I return to the table. He said I should not embarrass him. I didn't answer his calls, nor did I respond to the text. I walked out the door with the driver who took me home, and I never heard from Dr. Big Penis again. Choice Points had become easier to discern and were made almost instantaneously, because I had excavated, released conditioning, and was learning my value.

Choice Points can usher us into sharing ourselves by revealing who we are and grant us passage to speak our Truth. Choice Points in the beginning can be challenging, yet they are beneficial gifts. When we make choices from the evolution of ourselves instead of our conditioned self, we become fortified and develop character, which makes us content with our actions. We communicate to ourselves and others that we are magnificent, precious, unique, and a powerful woman. With one choice at a time, I became a woman who learned to value and honor myself. I learned and continue to learn how to reveal myself and share my voice. I went from an unexpressed girl to a person in a violent relationship to a woman who lives an expressive, peaceful, joyful, and fulfilling life. The journey from there to here wasn't easy, nor was it hard; it was a necessary and required commitment. And, without the seemingly difficult journey, I wouldn't be here at this majestic place in my life.

Please make a commitment to yourself to learn your value. Create a Life-of-Delight, make Self-Honoring Choices, and live each day with the Knowingness that *You Are the Prize*.

CHAPTER TWELVE

TELLING IT JUST LIKE IT IS

The first time I heard my husband's voice, it was over the phone, and I got butterflies in my belly. A few days later, when I met him face-to-face, the feeling of the butterflies returned and there was a sense of immediate, personal comfort with him. Our meeting was completely unexpected, yet there was so much synchronicity that needed to happen for us to have met. He had an appointment at my office to see a colleague. However, when he arrived, my colleague wasn't there, so I had to take the appointment. What I know today is that the moment he saw me, there was a recognition within him too. He also had butterflies in his belly.

Our first conversation lasted around forty-five minutes and had nothing to do with the business he came to discuss. We found out we shared interests in psychology and real estate. He had been a professor, chair of the psychology department, and participated in various arenas of real estate. I had recently finished a two-year master's program in spiritual psychology, and my entire working life had been in real estate. We both had the compulsion to be of service, and share time with our family and friends. When our conversation concluded, still no real estate business had been discussed, although I did give him a tour of the property. As he was ready to leave, I gave him my business card, and while giving him my business card, I heard my Inner Voice say, "Tell him it was nice chatting with you." My ego immediately took over and said, "No! Don't say that!" Before I knew it, the words expelled from my mouth, "It was nice chatting with you."

His reply, "It was nice chatting with you too. Perhaps we can continue this conversation. May I call you?"

"Yes," I responded.

He continued, "Shall I call you here at your office?"

"Yes, I would like that," I answered and off he went.

Later that afternoon, he called, and I have to say that from the time he left until the moment he called, I didn't have even one thought about him. It was almost as if we had never met. He was completely absent from my thoughts. However, when he called, the moment I heard his voice, I was filled with excitement. Our conversation was brief, and the only objective was to schedule a time and date to continue the chat which had begun earlier that day.

Later that evening, I was speaking to my god-sister and telling her about the fascinating man I'd chatted with earlier and I was going to meet to continue the conversation.

"Where are you going? When are you going?" were the two questions she asked.

After I responded to each of the questions, she replied, with a funny grin on her face, "Honey Girl, that's not continuing a conversation. That's a date."

It didn't occur to me until she said it. I was actually going on a date. I had suspended dating for months, and I wasn't thinking about dating at all, because each man I was meeting was not fulfilling my new criteria. In other words, my Choice Points had reached a level of discernment that, upon introduction and talking after a few moments, I was able to know clearly if I would proceed or stop the engagement. Choice Points give way to clarity.

Our first date could not have been more perfect. He arrived on time, handsomely attired, smelled good, and

I could sense his joy. When we approached the car, he opened the door, gave me the seatbelt, and gingerly closed the door. The car radio station was tuned to a classical setting that I often listen to. I knew we were going to have a very nice evening. His preparation for our time together was evidenced by the cleanliness of his car, his attire, the radio station, the restaurant selected, and even the table he reserved (which I was unaware of at that moment, but it conveyed his thoughtfulness). From my perspective, everything was a communication of the value he held for himself and the regard he had for me. When we arrived at the restaurant, the hostess commented on the joy she could see in our faces. Her comment made us both beam. We were escorted to the table, and from the moment we sat down until four and a half hours later, when I got up to go to the restroom, we were fully engaged with one another; of course, minus giving our server attention when necessary. When I got up to go to the ladies' room, I noticed that only a few people were left in the restaurant.

"Do you realize we're among the last ones here?" he asked when I returned to the table.

"I didn't until I got up to go to the restroom," I said.

I shared with him that there was a lady who remarked, "You and your husband haven't looked up from the table since you arrived. I was wondering what could you be talking about? My husband and I don't have that much to talk about ever." She smiled and departed from the ladies' room. I washed my hands with a smile on my face and across my heart, thinking, "Wow! She thinks he's my husband."

During our date, I introduced Stephen to the real me, RaShawn Renée. The woman who had learned to wholly accept herself, knew her value, and was aware she's the Prize. I told him big and little stuff about my life. I shared experiences that I once felt shame about, told him about my previous paradigm of being silent and hidden, and I even took my shoes off, sat with my feet under me, and ate with my hands. I let him see all of me and no longer felt the need to hide any of me.

I said, "I like the sensuality of food coming from my hands to my mouth. I enjoy experiencing the sensations of me."

I had never expressed myself in that manner before. It was as if sitting with him I was learning even more about myself. Everything I shared, he listened to with a face of acceptance and the energy of an open heart. It was apparent he had no judgments about anything I shared or did while at the restaurant. During dinner, I asked him to tell me something which he carried shame about and rarely, if ever, discussed. He was taken aback by the question. Yet after a pause, restating the question, and a sip of water, he answered. I listened attentively, looked at him through the eyes of acceptance, and heard him with an open heart. I too had no judgments about what he shared. I could not have dreamed of a better experience or desired anything to be different that evening. Our first date affirmed, by my outward actions and conversation, that I was no longer hiding. I felt safe; love, honor, and wholeness for myself; and I became aware of this on the first date with the extraordinary man who is now my husband.

On our second date, we discussed previous relationships, my choice to be celibate, and choosing not to share my body until I was in a committed relationship with the intention of marriage. I also communicated that it would be a minimum of three months of getting to know him to even consider having sex as part of our relationship. I was in a magnificent place when I met Stephen, and it didn't matter if he accepted or rejected my additional communication regarding the standards and criteria that had become my way of living. I was completely in acceptance of myself and making Self-Honoring Choices. I had learned, through a series of seemingly bumpy experiences, my value and I recognized that every relationship up until that point presented itself in my life so I could learn to wholly value myself. I was willing to use my complete life as my curriculum to learn me. Meaning I was no longer willing to make choices for the benefit of another, especially if they didn't honor me.

The most magnificent gifts I've given to myself are learning how to live and love. We owe ourselves the gift of real love and not just living a superficial connection and existing. We owe ourselves the gift of whole-self acceptance and not just pretending so we can fit in. It's time to move beyond conditioning and sequestered thinking, which is the thinking that keeps women in the mindset of survival, external images, and so-called security, which is also living superficial connections and existing. All of that keeps us away from experiencing the beauty of self-honor and self-awareness. Once conditioned thinking is no longer part of your paradigm, then self-discovery, gratitude, fulfillment, and love become perpetual experiences.

Are you ready to accept the magnificent gifts your life is offering?

What are your current experiences?

Are you fulfilled?

Are you sharing yourself wholly?

Not surprising, he respected my communication and concurred that we should take things slow between us. Each call and text message from the second, third, and fourth date was filled with our appreciation for one another and revealed our desires to continue getting to know each other. Then came an unexpected bombshell of disbelief. We met at a lovely hotel near the Pacific Ocean. The plan was to have a light late dinner, listen to live music, and relax. When I arrived at the hotel, Stephen was already there near the bar area and drank two cocktails prior to my arrival. This date was already different. A couple of times during our date I asked, "Are you OK?" His reply: "I'm OK." He never drank two cocktails at any point on our previous dates. On this date, he had two cocktails before I arrived and one and a half while on the date. When our date concluded, I observed Stephen wasn't steady in his footing, something I hadn't seen before. I insisted on driving him home, and he politely declined. I persisted until he accepted my invitation to drive him home. I wasn't going to allow a taxi, Uber, or a car service to drive him home; I cared for him and about his well-being. He was touched by my unrelenting insistence to drive him home. When we arrived at his apartment, it was as he had described: tidy, clean, a bachelor pad with an elliptical machine in the middle of the living room, and a big bed in the bedroom. He told me his housekeeper had been there earlier that day, which meant the sheets were clean. I felt comfortable being in his home, and I knew it was completely safe to share the same bed. He gave me a T-shirt and robe. I put them both on and got in the bed. He slept on the right side, closest to the door, and I on the left, closest to the balcony. Once in the bed, we both lay there for about five minutes, not saying a word, with our backs to one another.

"Are you awake?" he finally asked me.

"Yes, I am," I replied.

"I am very pleased by the way you took care of me this evening and showed me your concern," he said.

"You're welcome. It was my pleasure," I responded.

While talking, our body positions changed, and we ended up in the middle of the bed and face-to-face. This position brought the natural occurrence of one kiss, which turned into another kiss, which became multiple kisses. My body responded in the magical way bodies communicate when aroused.

I abruptly stopped kissing him, sat up in the bed and said, "You or I will have to sleep on the couch, because I am not sharing myself with you, as much as I would like to. We are still discovering one another."

This was another powerful defining moment and Choice Point. I took another stance contrary to my desires. I was dating a man I really cared about, and I wasn't concerned about the possible ramifications of my actions because I was standing firmly in the choice. I was honoring the commitment I had made to myself and communicated to him. My mind and body wanted to have sex; however, my commitment to Self was more important than my desires. I wasn't willing to break the trust I had created with myself, nor dilute my power or confuse him by changing something I said was very important to me. I got out of the bed, walked in the direction towards the living room with the notion of sleeping on the couch. He followed me into the living room and insisted that if anyone was going to be sleeping on the couch, it would be him. We talked for a while about staying committed to our words and the importance of the Self-Honoring Choice I made to be celibate. Eventually, we ended up back in the bed on opposite sides, holding hands until we fell asleep.

I awoke feeling like I had become a giant overnight because I experienced myself as the woman who was continuing to speak up for herself and making choices of personal power. I had continued to stay on the path of self-honor even when it would have been easy and understandable to veer from the path. I could have continued kissing, had sex, and made those actions OK. Instead, at this Choice Point, I chose to express what was in alignment with my power and value. I reflected that I'm a woman who chooses to be seen, heard, and understood. Choice Points allowed me to define the real me and no longer was my outward identification reflective of silence and not speaking up. Unconscious conditioning and being fearful of consequence or punitive actions were no longer part of my paradigm. I was living in the precious and divine space of being seen, heard, and understood.

✳ ✳ ✳ ✳

When Stephen awoke, he found me sitting on the couch in his T-shirt and robe while reading the newspaper. He had a grin on his face and sat in the chair to my left. The conversation began with his expression of gratitude for me driving him home. It flowed into a conversation about our mutual attraction and our desire to physically share our bodies. Then the "real" conversation came—the bombshell communication he wanted to share the evening prior while on our date. He told me what was on his mind and what made him drink the most he had ever drunk in one night. He shared how difficult the conversation was for him to have, and how he didn't want to hurt my feelings. I braced myself for what was to come next. The conversation continued with recapturing the fun we had on each date, our dynamic communication and attraction to one another, and all the things that made him smile whenever he thought of me. Every word he said made my heart happy; however, I knew he was soon to say something contrary or reveal something horrible.

"I don't want to have a committed relationship. I want a relationship to date and have sex with you exclusively, while having the option to date other women," he said with teary eyes.

"I encourage you to date as many women as you like," I told him. "I see you as a really wonderful man whom I am extremely compatible with and attracted to, and I overwhelmingly enjoy your company. Yet, our ideas of commitment and what we desire at this time are opposite," I responded.

I recapped a couple of the very special moments from our previous dates and then said, "I'm not willing to do what you want, so I guess this means I can't see you anymore. Would you please take me back to the hotel, so I may get my car?"

The ride to the hotel was quiet and uncomfortable, yet we held hands for most of the drive. I felt a moderate amount of sadness, although I knew I was making the right choice to no longer see him. I told myself, "If God brought this great guy into my life, and he isn't for me, then God will bring a man for me who is beyond my comprehension." God had to supersede what I had experienced with Stephen for me to say yes to the next man I would date. Stephen had shown himself as someone who had integrity, was thoughtful, honest, kind, and respectful of himself and me.

When we arrived at the hotel, I sat in the car and watched while Stephen took care of me. Meaning he gave the attendant the valet ticket, waited for the car to arrive, had a bottle of water placed in the car, and paid the fee. Once everything was done, he came to retrieve me. He opened the door, took my hand, escorted me to my car, and treated me exactly the way I wanted, expected, and enjoyed. I felt comfortable with him even as we ended our relationship. It was time to say goodbye, and before getting in my car, we exchanged a long embrace. I kissed him on the check, he kissed me on the forehead, I got in my car, took one last glance at him, and drove away. While driving, I felt the sadness of knowing we were no longer dating, and I felt an underlying exhilaration of being proud of myself. I knew I had made the choice that was self-honoring, although very difficult.

Throughout the day, I thought of him many times, and each time I thought of him, I reminded myself of the exhilarating feeling I had earlier when driving home, and it wasn't a feeling of sadness. I chose to focus on the exhilaration because that would empower me to let go of the sadness; otherwise, it would confuse me. It was my day off and instead of running errands and doing my usual chores, I decided to spend time with a dear friend and talk about Stephen. Her recommendation was that I date him because the more time he and I spent together, he would come to realize he preferred dating me over anyone else. In the past, I would have accepted her recommendation and been willing to play "that game."

It is the responsibility of every female to hold herself in a place of self-honor. It's a place that commands a Way-of-Being with yourself and communicates the respect and value you have for *You*.

The advice I was given was understandable to me, as it would be for millions of women, evidenced by the numbers of women fighting amongst others over a man. This was another Choice Point, and it gave me an opportunity to see that I was strengthening the character of the woman I was becoming and wanted to be (I didn't take action on her recommendation).

I was living within a new paradigm, which was constructed by examining my conditioning, whole-self acceptance, understanding my value, making Self-Honoring Choices, and living in my personal power. My new Way-of-Being revealed to me "I am the Prize!" Actually, I had always been the Prize, I just didn't know it and wasn't living it. Do you know, wherever you are in your life in this moment, you too are the Prize? If you are living in a manner that communicates anything other than you're the Prize, it's time to learn your real Truth.

※ ※ ※ ※

It was around 8:00 p.m., the evening after the bombshell conversation, when Stephen called. He asked if we could have dinner the following night. I declined. Then he asked for the day after that. I also declined and reminded him that we were no longer dating, and although he could call me from time to time, I wasn't going out with him.

I said, "There is no need to share time with you. I want to share my time and energy with someone who wants to mutually explore a committed relationship in a manner that fits with mine."

He said passionately, "I changed my mind about dating other women after thinking about this all day."

I wasn't moved by his urgency to date me. From my perspective, this was a reactionary response and easily expected because of our fondness for one another.

I replied, "Give yourself a couple of days. See how you feel, and then if you don't want to date other women, I will be willing to meet you."

Before hanging up the phone, we made a "just-in-case date" for the end of the following week. He called three days later to confirm that he still didn't want to date other women, and we met each other for our date. The moment I saw him, I had butterflies in my belly again like when I first heard his voice. I felt a sense of greater tranquility being in his presence. I was ecstatic he had decided that he didn't want to date other women. I was pleased to be sitting across from him and grateful I had learned I am the Prize.

The conversations we shared on that date were transformative and it bonded us. By the end of our date, we made an agreement to be in a committed relationship. We began creating our ideal scene for making love approximately three months from then. The clock was ticking, and we knew if things continued lovingly in our relationship, we would make love, be in a superlative relationship, and possibly marry.

* * * *

My sexual innocence was stolen; I gave my virginity to a boyfriend because he and others told me I should (it was time). Most of my sexual experiences had stemmed from perceived obligation and other familial and societal conditioning. Life was now completely different. I had chosen celibacy for more than four years, so I could learn and connect with myself intimately. Now I was planning to share my body, heart, and mind with a man because it was exactly what I wanted to do. I had become sexually educated in a way that promoted, embraced, and communicated the value of intimacy. I had learned what respect, honor, and cherishing meant to have for myself and be given to me by another. If everything went according to plan, I was soon to end years of celibacy and share myself in a way that would be honoring, fulfilling, and what Stephen and I would call an experience of heaven on earth.

* * * *

> Ladies, we are the Prize.
>
> Your sexuality is a gift, and each person you decide to share yourself with needs to recognize your value.
>
> You are the Prize.

Time seemed to pass quickly, and before we knew it, the day arrived to begin planning our trip and experience our ideal scene. Stephen knew the environment was an important part of the experience. So, when planning, he asked a few questions.

"Where would you like to go? Would you prefer to travel north or south? Do you have a particular destination of where we will cocoon for five days?"

Instead of giving him the answers, which I could have easily done, I thought he should decide.

He said, "I think it should be a collaborative effort because that's the way we are building our relationship."

As we shared in the planning, one of the details was to select a hotel. He gave me three options. The first option he gave was a hotel I had wanted to go to ever since I saw it in a travel magazine more than a decade prior. I remember thinking when I first saw the hotel, "One day I'll go here with my husband." While planning the trip, it became evident we were going to experience more than an ideal scene, a different state of heaven on earth. I was being cherished, honored, and valued by another, and I would soon experience something beyond my wildest dreams. In part, it was happening because I learned to give myself what I was now receiving from another.

The last-minute details had been taken care of by Stephen before we arrived at the hotel. We only had to wait a few minutes before we could go to our suite. About ten minutes after arriving, we were standing at the end of a hallway in front of double doors. I rang the doorbell just for fun, and to my surprise, the door opened. As I walked in, the visual feast before me was intoxicating. Our suite was perched on a hillside with an ocean view. The appointment to every detail was obvious and exquisite. The décor was inviting, comfortable, and luxurious. There were two large relaxation chairs and a table. Prominently displayed on the table was an overwhelming floral arrangement, which consisted of orchids, roses, lilies, tulips, and a host of other flowers I don't even know the names of. The aroma from the flowers filled the room. When the bellman left, I went to the floral arrangement to breathe in one of the Sterling roses commanding my attention. While breathing in the fragrance, Stephen, who was standing next to me, reached into his jacket pocket and gave me a card.

"Darling, I wanted you to have a bouquet that's almost

as beautiful as you are, and I realized it isn't possible, so I hope this will do."

"You're wonderful!" were the words written on the card. While reading the card, tears rolled down my face. Stephen put his arms around me, and while in his arms, I was even more aware; I am the Prize. The tears went from crying to almost sobbing because I was aware my life had been forever changed. I was aware I was valuable, and I wholly accepted myself. I was also aware that Stephen recognized my value. Yes! This moment was heaven on earth. The discovery of Self had brought me to that point in my life. There I was in a beautiful suite with a remarkable man, having excavated, examined, and released the conditioning that didn't support me.

With the knowledge that a man isn't able to cherish and have esteem for a woman until she has it for herself, I recognize I wasn't able to have the partnership of my dreams until I learned to be a dream for myself.

A man isn't able to honor you until you honor yourself. A man can't value you unless you value yourself.

And once you value yourself, when you decide to be with a man, he has to earn you.

Life becomes more beautiful and fulfilling when you know...you're the Prize. It's not from an ego state of knowing, it's from the intrinsic state of your Being.

A lifetime of experiences, familial and societal conditioning, coupled with allowance of men (some women) to suppress, diminish, and render me silent are no longer present. Every experience is now used for my personal power and greater understanding. So at this point, I can share and teach women how to stand in their power, make Self-Honoring Choices, and understand their real Truth—you're the Prize. It's time for you to say yes to yourself because you deserve to live fully and love wholly.

The day I met my husband, I learned one of the greatest lessons from listening to my Still Small Voice. I was aware our Inner Guidance is always communicating with us, and God constantly presents opportunities for us to grow through ease and grace or hardship and pain. We can accept the path that nurtures and blossoms us through love, or we can choose to suffer by abandoning our True Self and grow through pain. If I didn't listen to my Inner Guidance and say, "It was nice chatting with you," (although it's not what I wanted to do) when Stephen was about to depart after our first meeting, I may have passed, missed, or delayed the experience of being fully embraced. Meaning I get to fully be myself and am encouraged to make choices that support my intrinsic value. Until I knew differently, I didn't listen to my Inner Knowing, and there was always suffering with punitive consequences. It's completely up to us how long we choose punitive consequences and suffering, and when we choose to be nurtured through grace and blossom into the magnificence we are. We all have the opportunity each day to live a life of privilege. Meaning you are cherished, appreciated, valued, and loved. I learned to live "this life" as a result of knowing all of those things for myself, and then it was given to me by another and another and another. And it continues when you choose YOU first!

My desire, journey, education, and knowledge give me the fortitude to support other women on their journey by supporting them to excavate and examine conditioning and learn the real Truth of who they are.

❈ ❈ ❈ ❈

Allison is an incredible woman. She has two children, is divorced, and has returned to college in her fifties. This lady doesn't allow anything to stand in the way of achieving her dreams. She sits on the board for an organization that empowers women and does a tremendous amount of philanthropic work. She is brilliant, dynamic, and beautiful! Allison badly wanted a romantic relationship and had been on numerous dating sites trying to find Mr. Right. She met a few men who intrigued her, whom she dated, and the relationships all ended rather quickly. One day while talking, she asked my opinion of her dating experiences and the way she was meeting men. I wanted to respond, yet I was sensitive to hurting her feelings.

I asked, "May I have a candid conversation with you, and will you be able to accept what I am going to say for your benefit and not think I'm judging you?"

She nodded in agreement and said, "Yes. Please tell me everything. Don't hold anything back. I can handle it."

I had known Allison since we were eight years old, so I had decades of observations and experiences to draw the parallels of how the conditioning of her upbringing was still dominating the way she related to men, herself, and every area of her life. I began the conversation by explaining her overall conditioning with men. Then I asked a series of questions, so she could begin to see how her conditioning was formed.

"At what age did you first have sex?"

"What was your first sexual encounter?"

"Why did you choose to have sex for the first time?"

"Was your first sexual encounter chosen or something else?"

"Who was the first man you admired and why?"

"Why and how did your first love relationship end?"

"Who taught you how to relate to men?"

"Who taught you how to model a relationship with a man?"

She was intrigued by the inquiries and ecstatic by the revelations she made for herself. By the conclusion of our conversation, I agreed I would assist Allison through her maze of dating and support her in releasing her unconscious conditioning. Since having a romantic relationship was at the top of her to-do list, I decided to begin with what was most important to her. The first step was to narrow down the sites she was on; the second was to change her profile picture and the description of what she was looking for. One week after completing steps one and two, she met the man of her dreams. According to him, he too met the woman he had dreamed of but thought didn't exist. From her first communication with him, I was guiding her to make Self-Honoring Choices and encouraging her to reveal herself truthfully.

I said, "You can say, 'I want to be married again and profoundly in love with my husband. I want a never-ending honeymoon.'"

The beginning of their telephone courtship took place while he was traveling out of the country. He was so interested in getting to know her that he made his schedule accommodate her request (actually my request). The call schedule was 5:30 p.m. PST on Tuesday, Thursday, and Saturday. After about two weeks of calls between them, he insisted he needed more phone time. She agreed, and they began talking every day. I made the recommendation she continue to keep the calls between thirty and forty-five minutes, which she was currently doing.

She disagreed and said, "If he wants more time, then I'm going to give him more time."

So she talked to him for hours whenever time permitted.

When he returned to the States, she wanted to pick him up at the airport and allow that to be part of their first date. I disagreed and recommended she wait at least one day after he returned home. She vehemently disagreed but haphazardly followed my recommendations. Jim was kind, philanthropic, wealthy, and worked very hard for his material and moral success. His dream was to find a wife to share his life with.

He said, "I have everything I have ever wanted except for someone to share it with, and I'm at the place in my life where all I want is to share all I have with someone very special."

He wanted to travel, have fun, and assist in making his wife's dreams come true. They planned their first date two days after he returned, at his request, not hers. He told her he was going to make an exception and pick her up without his driver because he wanted to be alone with her. I thought that was sweet, yet recommended against it.

I said, "Have him do what is usual. Allow his driver to pick you up."

My recommendation at this point landed on deaf ears. Her perception was she must be special if he wanted to pick her up without his driver. And so he picked her up without his driver. According to her, it was the best first date ever, and she couldn't wait for the second date. The day after their first date, he didn't call. She was disappointed and made the excuse that he was probably busy at work and unable to call. Well, of course that didn't make any sense, since he called her from Europe, as scheduled, while on his business trip for almost a month.

The second day after their first date, he called late in the evening. It was almost midnight, and he asked her for a second date. Early Friday morning, she and I met for a hike. She told me about the call the evening prior and communicated he wasn't as enthused as he had been on previous calls. After listening to Allison for most of the hike—she made every excuse imaginable for his pull-back behavior—I asked questions and discovered Allison had done almost everything possible to show she wasn't valuable and definitely she wasn't the Prize (everything against my recommendations).

Allison had passionately kissed him, sat on his lap at the restaurant, and talked about having sex with him, all on the first date. After she completed her story of...*I'm not the Prize*, I said, "In the beginning, you were doing things the way I guided and everything was going perfectly. Now you've done everything your way, via conditioning, and perhaps you're ready now to act again based upon my guidance."

She nodded in agreement. I continued the conversation by reiterating what I had said in the past.

"Just because he was your dream man over the phone, you need his actions to mirror his verbal communications. Just because he felt like driving you himself on your first date in no way meant you were special. It only conveyed that he wanted to be alone with you perhaps to see how easily you could be seduced or any one of a myriad of reasons which wouldn't include you're special. You have no way of knowing who he is by mere communications over the phone."

I said that and much more. After a long monologue by me, I gave her the information necessary to remedy the damage from the first date. In other words, I gave her the template for a successful second date and more. The second date was going along perfectly, according to Allison. She took all recommendations and he responded with the enthusiasm of their previous communications while at the restaurant. One of the recommendations in the template was limited physical contact, such as touching and caressing. On this date, there was to be no passionate kissing. The date concluded with Jim taking Allison to his sparsely furnished waterfront home in a private community. The house sat on almost an acre of land, and Jim shared with Allison he designed that home for his future wife. According to Allison, he said, "I built this for her. She's going to furnish it, and perhaps you are that woman. That's why I brought you here." Allison wanted to be "that woman," and she wanted to prove herself worthy of his dream. So instead of leaving and allowing him to learn her value, she decided to have sex with him and give him her non-value. After that night, Allison never heard from Jim again.

Here's a question for all of us. If a man has worked diligently to get where he is in life, wouldn't it be reasonable for him to have to work diligently for the woman with whom he wants to share his life? Ladies, when you know you're the Prize, men want to be in your company. Men want to be around you, because it reveals to them the attributes of a woman who honors herself. Every man wants a woman who values herself because it communicates to him she can value him. If he is a man who desires an all-encompassing and fulfilling life, then he knows he has to have a woman who honors herself. It is true, *"Behind every good man is a great woman."*

A real man comes into your life to serve, take care of, and support you while assisting you in discovering more about yourself and blossoming into all you can be. Men want to be our heroes, and they want us to be their Prize. Being the Prize resides within you. Perhaps you've just covered it up by your conditioning, limited thinking, and societal conformity. You don't have to give your body, share your sexuality, give your time, or in any way be intimate with a man until you're ready.

Here is a statement of truth and power, and rarely said: your vagina is one of the wonders of the world. I say our vaginas are a utopia. Meaning they are beautiful and created for great pleasure and to continue society. It is probably the most sought-after "treasure" in the world desired by the masses and it's priceless. If you're a woman who commonly communicates your affection through your vagina with the hope of securing love, there is a great distance from you knowing your Truth that you are the Prize. Learn, then live as the woman you truly are. You are magnificent. You are priceless. You are the Prize!

No matter where you are at this moment, use every experience for your learning.

CHAPTER THIRTEEN

IT'S UP TO YOU

I was stopped by a sense of peace that was omnipresent, and within this peaceful state, I was also aware of bliss and fulfillment. "What is this?" I rhetorically asked my husband.

Within a nanosecond, he replied, "It's ecstasy, sweetheart."

I felt my body breathe in his response and knew what he said was the truth. I was experiencing ecstasy. Wow! It was a new feeling, and it was produced by the culmination of making choices from self-learning, listening to the Still Small Voice, forgiving, loving, and honoring myself and others. This was the journey; the journey wasn't easy, but it was necessary.

Each of us wants to know we matter. We want to be cherished, appreciated, and valued by another. Every one of us has had moments when we know the life we're living isn't the fullest expression of who we are, nor are we living the life we truly desire. In life, there comes a time when taking a deeper inquiry into yourself by learning who you really are becomes an inner call that needs to be answered. If you're willing, this is your time. The life of self-honor, personal power, fulfillment, perpetual joy, and ecstasy awaits you.

Are you ready?

I'm so grateful I learned to make Self-Honoring Choices and now know the feeling of ecstasy. Once upon a time, I watched my life spiral downward in a way that left me with only two options: to continue to go down the abyss of my conditioning, or to discover the Truth of who I am through excavation. Like millions of women conditioned by the cycle of family and society, it was difficult to make a choice outside of the normal paradigm. I have learned to make choices from my Truth and I no longer react to life from unexamined conditioning which has given me personal power. I'm asking you to do the same. It is a great gift to learn who You are and to know your Truth. I didn't know I could choose me, and by choosing me, it gave me the ability to create a life that was more inclusive. It guided me to everything I've ever desired. What are you choosing? How are you choosing to live? What do you desire? Are you ready to create a Life-of-Delight? Are you ready to know ecstasy? If you aren't certain you're ready, then ask yourself these questions:

Do I pretend I've got it all together?

Do I often compare myself to and judge others?

Am I so far away from myself I can no longer see me clearly? Meaning, is the life you're living beneath the vision you once had for yourself?

Am I living my life as I choose or the life someone else has crafted for me to live?

If you responded yes to any of those questions, then you're ready to begin or to continue the exploration of you.

This beautiful, yet seemingly complex journey of learning yourself, independent of your conditioning, is expansively revelatory, because it offers every experience you've ever had in life to be part of your learning. Therefore, the whole of your life becomes your curriculum, and each experience is beneficial to your current moment. The learning of Self becomes your personal reference book, and your life is the content of that book. From the moment you say "Yes" to yourself and allow your actions to reflect the truth of who you are, your life begins to change almost instantly. To understand yourself, make Self-Honoring

Choices, and live day-to-day experiences of fulfillment and perpetual joy: these are available to you once you learn your Truth and live in your Power. A friend said to me, "Your journey is a manifesto for all of us; you took the bullet, so we don't have to." I completely appreciated her acknowledgment for my journey, and yet, I see it a little differently than she does. I didn't take a bullet. I moved from the range of the bullet, metaphorically speaking. Meaning my story is part of my life curriculum and reflects, in part, the Choice Points I made prior in life that kept me in the line of fire. Meaning when I was making choices that led me to a violent relationship, that too was part of my learning. Had I not had that experience, I may never have reached the point of such desperation where I was willing to abandon everything to find me. My line of fire, as yours, comes from unexamined conditioning. Whatever choices you are making at this time that don't support the life you want to create come from conditioning that you have yet to examine. Are you ready to begin excavating and learning about yourself?

The other part of my story reveals Choice Points, which demonstrate the power of making Self-Honoring Choices, choosing not to hide, having whole-self acceptance, and seeing the Truth of who I am. It is my desire that this story becomes part of your story. I want you to choose to move out of the range of fire so you can begin to live the life that is calling you forward. Do you know the story of *The*

Hero's Journey? It's the journey we each take when we let go of limited thinking and existing and move into living a life of self-honor and fulfillment. Are you ready to take your journey and become a hero? I know you desire to be heard, seen, and know you matter. We all do. It's part of our human design, and this could be your time to live fully and to know what it feels like to be pleased with yourself, proud of you, not from your ego-self, from your soul, and to continue stepping into the life you know you want to live. You can do it! Isn't it time to stop living marginally, being afraid, and hiding yourself? Wouldn't it be great to honor yourself and give yourself the life you know you can have? I want you to know the feeling of peace, to attune to your Inner Guidance, to know the promptings of the Still Small Voice, to learn yourself and have the fulfilling and miraculous life you were born to experience. This is your time to begin or continue on your *hero's journey*. Remember, the life you're creating isn't a destination, it's an accumulation of personal riches acquired moment-by-moment based upon your choices. As you take this journey and begin creating a Life-of-Delight, Choice Points will be your constant compass, and you will begin living a life that is unimaginable at this moment. This is your time.

❋ ❋ ❋ ❋

I grabbed my keys, rushed out the door, and headed to the local hardware store to get plant food for my newly planted bougainvillea. I was gardening that afternoon, something I rarely do and really enjoy. I pulled into the parking garage, and after driving around twice, I realized this was going to take a bit longer than I'd expected because there were no parking spaces available. I went around the third time, and I noticed there was a parking space becoming available. When I arrived there, another car was waiting. So I patiently sat behind the car hoping another space would open, and it did. After about two minutes, I noticed a woman walking to her car, which was about four spaces ahead. She got in her car and began pulling out. As she backed out, I maneuvered around the car in front of me and began pulling into the space. As I was pulling into the spot, the woman that I was previously behind sped up in an attempt to take the space.

She began yelling, "You fucking bitch! I was waiting for that parking place! Who do you think you are?"

As she raged on with her pejoratives, I didn't feel anger or the necessity to react. Instead, I felt compassion for her. I knew the reason she was reacting that way had absolutely nothing to do with me. She didn't know me, and clearly, there was no reason for her to be enraged over a parking space that she wasn't waiting for.

I rolled down the window completely and said very calmly, "That's not the parking space you were waiting for. It appears the car you were waiting for still hasn't backed out. So, I will give you this parking space, and I recommend you calm down, because if you don't, you're going to have a really bad day."

With tears in her eyes, she said, "Now I feel like a bitch. You take the parking place. I don't want it."

While insisting she take the parking space, another spot opened, and she drove off to park there. As she was parking, my Inner Guidance told me to wait for her to park and speak to her. However, I didn't want to do what I heard. I tried to convince myself I wasn't hearing accurately. Finally, I stopped trying to find my way out of what I was being guided to do. I waited for her to exit her vehicle. When she got out of the car, I approached her, introduced myself, and said, "I recommend you change your attitude because if you don't, you're going to have a very bad day, and whatever is going on in your world, it's no need for you to lash out at me or anyone else. You may curse at the wrong person."

She began crying uncontrollably and told me the story of the guy she wanted to date for months who had finally invited her on a date. She had been preparing for a week to make certain she looked especially good when they went out, and he had just canceled the date only a few hours prior to them meeting.

She said, "He's never going to be with someone who looks as good as me."

She was about twenty-seven years old, and it was obvious she had made cosmetic investments in her body. Her hair, nails, makeup, and outfit were esthetically pleasing. She was very nicely put together on the outside. I talked to her in the garage for about twenty-five to thirty minutes. During our conversation, I asked the questions that would aid me in discovering where the conditioning of only identifying herself from her physical appearance stemmed from. Through questioning and her responses, I learned when she was fourteen she won the votes to be student body president by one vote, and according to the election rules, the president had to win by at least three votes. The class voted to recast their ballots the following day. The next day, when she returned to school, she was called into the office and told she should focus on her academics because she was an A student and her grades may suffer with the additional responsibility of being president of the student council. She assured the faculty member she wouldn't allow her position to interfere with her grades. The more she tried to convince the faculty member of her commitment to maintain her almost 4.0 GPA, the more the faculty member persisted in his communication. Finally, the faculty member said something like, "You should be prettier, not smarter. Your looks will take you further than your brain. You don't need to be student body president; your classmate does. Men are leaders."

The woman who had just cursed me out over a parking space was weeping uncontrollably and sharing the defining moment where she decided to hide herself. That day she chose to begin being more concerned with her looks than her brain.

"Everyone around me seemed to welcome the change. When I stopped being smart, people liked me more, especially the boys. When I stopped reading a lot, even more people started to like me," she confessed.

We concluded our conversation with a long embrace and, "Thank you very much for listening to me and talking to me. I'm really sorry for cursing at you. I didn't mean anything I said, and the parking spot was really yours. I just wanted it," she told me.

I gave her a kiss on the cheek after we finished our hug and responded, "Start reading again. Don't go out with that guy, and you've got to learn you and then really love you."

She smiled. "I don't know if I love myself. You're right. Thank you," she said.

Then out of nowhere came a girl styled and cosmetically

portioned in the same manner as the woman I was speaking with.

"Where the fuck have you been? I've been waiting for you," said her friend.

"Remembering I like to read and I'm smart," she said to her friend.

"Please remember our conversation," I reminded her and exited the parking garage.

I was being a Mother-to-Another. Women, this is what you must do for one another while excavating and when learning who You are. Once you know you're the Prize, we must continue to support each other until we all know the Truth and Power of ourselves. We are all the Prize.

The power of woman is incomparable to *no thing* in humanity. We are the gift of creation. We perpetuate existence, and without us, society would end, and mankind would become extinct. We are among the greatest assets on the planet, and yet most of us don't know our Truth or Power. We diminish our own value. We invalidate one another and cause strife amongst our fellow women. Let's stop this paradigm and step into our personal power. Excavate, learn, and release what doesn't serve you. Forgive, accept, and love the whole of you! Be a Mother-to-Another until each one of us is living a fulfilling life created by Self-Honoring Choices. It is time to release the tentacles of conditioned thinking and live in the magnificent manifestation of the woman you are. You are the Prize! The time for hiding yourself is over. It's time to wholly accept and express *you*.

Once you know who you are, you will begin seeing the emergence of your character developing. Prior to excavating and learning your real Truth, you recognize your choices were made from reactionary and conditioned responses. Therefore, your character wasn't developed; it was manufactured through your conditioning. When you learn the Truth and Power of Self, your choices are birthed from your intrinsic knowing, which commands self-honor. The standards you impose upon yourself as you live in this new paradigm will clearly define, develop, and exhibit your true character. You are magnificent!

I attended a funeral with my uncle, and after the service, while walking to the car, a man my uncle knew asked if he could ride back to the hotel with us. My uncle said yes, and the man joined us as we walked to the car. When we got there, my uncle went to the driver's side, opened his door and said to his friend, "Would you please open the door for my niece? She won't get in the car unless you open her door."

David just stood there as if he hadn't heard a word my uncle said, and I too stood there waiting for the door to be opened. My uncle repeated himself, and then David responded, "I don't open the car door for any capable woman."

My uncle and he had a circuitous exchange for about a minute or two while I listened, observed, and patiently waited for someone to open my door. Eventually, my uncle came to open the door for me. One of the many things I learned when I began to see myself clearly was I recognized I enjoy having men open the door for me. Although that was part of my conditioning, I kept it in my new paradigm because it's one of my standards.

So, whenever I approach the door, and there's a man within my proximity, I pause and offer the man an opportunity to support his nature (remember, most men enjoy opening the door for you). While driving to the hotel, I asked my uncle's friend, "What woman made you decide not to be a gentleman anymore? I can tell that's what you really are."

David gave me a blank stare, and I restated the question, "How did she break your heart, and when did it happen?"

After a long pause, as if he were waiting for me to ask another question, he sighed and began communicating. David recounted the story of the first woman he loved; he expressed the things he did for her, and one of those things was opening the door. He declared not only did it make him feel like a gentleman, it made him happy because it pleased her so much. We talked the entire time riding back to the hotel. David conveyed his unconditional love for her and his desire to be different than her philandering father and other men who had betrayed her.

He said, "I wanted to be her hero." David shared their dreams and the painful details of their breakup.

"She didn't mean to hurt you. She was only operating from what she knew, and obviously, she didn't know how to honor herself, or she wouldn't have broken your heart by having an affair."

When a woman knows herself and her value, she will simply end the relationship and move on. It leaves little residue.

"Her response to you was impersonal. It was her unexamined conditioning that prompted her affair," I shared.

"Although the relationship ended over nine years ago, I have been thinking and feeling I wasn't good enough for her. I never thought about her conditioning or mine," he agonizingly responded.

I continued the conversation by contributing, "When a

man or any person continues to do something against their nature, they gradually reach a point when they become unrecognizable to themselves in terms of their behavior. Subconsciously, the individual is telling themselves, in your case, you're not good enough. Then little by little, you push yourself away from your power. Meaning, subconsciously, it's affirmed to you that you don't matter, have no value, and aren't good enough, so you become more of who you aren't."

This tall, athletic, and seemingly, at first glance, emotionally tough guy began fighting back his tears. The communication I expressed to him was deeply touching; he felt the Truth in what I was saying. Our conversation began his excavation.

When we arrived at the hotel, I had a new buddy, and we spent about another hour talking in the lobby before going up to our rooms. By the time we concluded our conversation, David was determined to reclaim his power by revealing himself as the kind, openhearted gentleman he was instead of masquerading as an indifferent, callous man.

Men and woman have to reveal themselves.

Say YES! and rid what doesn't create a Life-of-Delight.

Later that evening, while at dinner with about seven other people, my uncle observed David and said, "You look like a different man."

"I look like myself. You've only seen me as that other man. Right now, I'm feeling like myself, again. Your niece really helped me," he said.

David glanced towards me at the table, gave me a wink, then got up, walked to my seat and said, "May I pull out your chair and give you a hug?"

When he spoke, I could sense he was different than a few hours prior. I felt his tenderness.

I responded, "Of course you can give me a hug."

He pulled out my chair and gave me a compassionate embrace; as we embraced, everyone at the table began clapping. I think everyone saw and felt him reveal his True Self. Everyone gets to see himself or herself and make Self-Honoring Choices when they're ready. Each of us has the capacity to live our Truth, create a Life-of-Delight, learn from our experiences, wholly accept ourselves, and make Self-Honoring Choices when we decide.

My story has evolved into a Life-of-Delight in which I make Self-Honoring Choices, see myself clearly, and treat myself with adoration while knowing my value. Every experience in your life can be used to benefit you if you allow it. As a child, my sexual innocence was hijacked. As a woman, I was arrested and slept with a hammer under the bed to protect myself. In the gap, I was trying to figure "it" out. Meaning I existed from day to day, really not knowing anything because I had yet to learn me. Now I awake feeling peaceful in the arms of my husband who prays for me and over us before we get out of bed each morning.

As a girl, I was shuffled back and forth between my parents' and grandparents' homes. As a woman, I heard more than one man say, "this is your home." The feeling of home eluded me, and I never felt secure in any of those houses. Today, I live in a home and all I feel here is LOVE! I once felt invisible and perpetually went against my Inner Guidance. Now I am attuned to the Still Small Voice and follow the guidance given me, which continually creates a life where I get to daily reveal myself, share my voice, and be fully seen. I once was too ashamed to call my mother and brother. Now we speak almost daily and share the gamut of our experiences and emotions. Each day I awake feeling blessed to be living the life I finally said YES to!

It's time to reveal yourself and learn the Truth of who you are by excavating and examining your conditioning. It is my absolute desire that you make the choice to create a Life-of-Delight through Self-Honoring Choices so that each day when you awake, you are aware of the magnificence You are.

There are no accidents or coincidences; this book is in your hands on purpose.

I know you're ready to experience a different love relationship with yourself.

To LOVE yourself because you're a magnificent creation.

To love yourself as the unique expression You are.

To love yourself because you're making Self-Honoring Choices.

To love yourself knowing every experience is beneficial.

To love yourself because you're sharing the Truth.

To love yourself wholly exactly as you are.

To love yourself because you're *You*.

This is your time.

YOU'RE THE PRIZE!

Dearest Reader,

Now that you have finished reading, please go to the next page of this book (where indicated), extract the note and send or give it, along with the book to someone that would benefit from reading it.

Dearest _____

You are receiving this note because we want to make a deposit of Love into your life...WOW! Doesn't it feel good to know that you're being thought of and cared about?

As you read 44 Hours & 21 Minutes: A Woman's Truth and Power, remember:

- You matter and that's why this letter is in your hand.
- This is your time to live the magnificence that You are!
- You are the Prize!

This is a Love Note from RaShawn Renée and me. We hope that you will allow this book to be a useful tool to aid you in learning more about You!

Only Love,

_____ & RaShawn Renée

I drdrtebect Wont

ACKNOWLEDGMENTS

I'm grateful!

Thank you, God, for bringing me into existence.

Thank you, parents, for giving me life.

Thank you, my cherished aunts, uncles, nieces, nephews, and cousins for being my family and sharing love.

Thank you, friends who have become family, for your inspiration, encouragement, and support.

Thank you, to each person who has held my hand to the completion of *44 Hours & 21 Minutes: A Woman's Truth and Power*.

Thank you, to every person who contributed to the stories contained in the pages of this book.

Thank you, MamaGirl, Brother, Sister, CocoPop, LX, LL, and Honey for our sacred sharings, choosing, and profound love.

Thank you, Sweetie and Bou for your daily deposits of whatever is required to nurture my heart.

Thank you, to Sloane and Jackson for coming into my life, adding another purpose and more joy.

Thank you, my Forever Love, for loving me wonderfully, spectacularly, being beyond my dream and praying for me and over us, each day.

information can be obtained
v.ICGtesting.com
i in the USA
7031717220119
809LV00001B/117/P